The Love of Lotus

Cynthia Waiying Wu Wilcox

Tyde House Books
Redwood City, California

www.theloveoflotus.com
www.tydehousebooks.com

Design and composition by
Scott Perry
Berkeley, California

Cover photo by
Robert Harrington

Published by
Tyde House Books
Redwood City, California

Printed in the United States of America

Publisher's Cataloging-in-Publication
(Provided by Quality Books, Inc.)

Wilcox, Cynthia Waiying Wu.
   The love of lotus / Cynthia Waiying Wu Wilcox.
   p. cm.
   LCCN 2006904407
   ISBN-13: 978-0-9786135-8-7
   ISBN-10: 0-9786135-8-9

   1. Wilcox, Cynthia Waiying Wu. 2. Chinese American
women--Biography. 3. Chinese Americans--Social life and
customs. 4. China--Intellectual life--1912-1949.
5. China--Social life and customs.   I. Title.

E184.C5W545 2006   973'.04951'0092
                           QBI06-600093

For

My Son, Jon Anthony,

My Grandchildren, Maya and Alejandro,

and

My Twenty-Five Nieces and Nephews

Love of Lotus
by Chou Dunyi (1017-1073)

Of all the plants that grow on land and in water, there are many one can love. In the Chun dynasty, Tao Yunming chose the chrysanthemum. Since the Tang dynasty, people have much preferred peonies. I love the lotus for its character: growing out of the mud and not being sullied, cleansing itself in the clear water and not being proud. Its stems are hollow inside and straight outside, lofty and unbranching. The fragrance of its flowers spreads wide — the farther, the more delicate. Its flowers stand alone, tall and elegant. One should enjoy only from afar, without cutting or plucking them.

I say the chrysanthemum is the flower of the solitary, the peony is the flower of the wealthy, and the lotus is the flower of the gentlemanly.

Alas, the love of the chrysanthemum is seldom mentioned after Tao Yunming. As for the love of the lotus, who are with me? The love of the peony, that is for the common people.

THIS ESSAY WAS the first one I understood after I enrolled in grade school. When we began schooling, we memorized many poems and ancient texts. I can still recite them. But I did not comprehend the meaning of the texts that mentioned patriotism, showed longings and romantic love for a woman, or touched other adult topics. This one discussed the essence of character, the core of a being. Somehow, I began to understand that it was important to retain and improve one's character and not let the outside world "sully" it. This was the beginning of my inner self.

CWW, December 2005
Woodside, California

Contents

Acknowledgments

THIS BOOK WAS STARTED some time ago when my son, Jon Anthony, asked me how I grew up in China. He had no idea of what it was like and couldn't even imagine it. I thank him for giving me the idea for the book. He and his wife, Tania, read the manuscript, contributing ideas as I proceeded.

Not long after my son's query, in late 1994 the Radcliffe Peninsula Alumni Writing Group was formed and I was invited to join. The six original members were: Libby Codd, the late Betsy Crowder, Virginia Herbert, the late Kitty Hislop, Ethel Meece and myself. We met once a month and discussed what we had written. Each member took turns in reading her writing. I benefited immensely from this group of understanding friends.

Later, Elizabeth Burgard, Madeline Crowley, Cassandra Moore and Lucy Savage joined the group off and on. The most persistent attendee was Madeline Crowley, who published her memoir *Call To Rise* soon after she joined us. Her enthusiasm and encouragement kept me going.

The next book published by members of the group was Ethel Meece's *Listening to The Rain Crow*. Ethel coached me, edited my writing and showed me the steps to publishing. Without her guidance, this book would not be in print.

Friends Ed Klingman and Ruth Nemzoff, my niece May

Leung and her husband Richard read the manuscript at its early, unruly stage and made valuable contributions.

My brother Yingchou and sister Waitung read the manuscript and made suggestions concerning historical accuracy. Their suggestions that I should publish the book were the final impetus to the project.

My editor, Polly Tooker, painstakingly read and edited the entire manuscript several times, enabling me to present this book with confidence. A better editor I could not find.

The one who tiredlessly tended to the editing and publishing details was my husband, Jonathan, who as usual, encouraged, cajoled and pushed me to finish the task. I thank him for his love and patience.

CWW
Woodside, CA

Preface

HEAT AND HUMIDITY engulfed the village of Pokfulam, on the edge of Hong Kong. Not even the usual breeze blew through the narrow lanes this afternoon of August 7, 1929. A young man scurried by, vegetable-filled baskets swaying from ends of a bamboo pole balanced on his shoulder, his bare feet slapping on the unpaved path. Scents of salt-preserved fish drying under eaves mixed with the sour odor of open sewage, smells sharply separating the village from the diesel fumes of the highway along the north side. In front of thatched roof huts, old men sat talking, fanning themselves lazily. A young mother chasing her toddler called out for the child to stop. Roosters, ducks, pigeons and pigs wandered in and out of lanes here and there. There was no sense of urgency in this crowded Southern tropical village.

In a small brick house down the street from the highway, a midwife tended a young woman in the bedroom. Beads of sweat rolled down the pale face of the expectant mother as she moaned, turning her head from side to side. The midwife gently urged the laboring woman to push harder: "The baby is coming!"

With a loud cry, the baby emerged. The midwife carefully cleaned the baby before carrying the small creature, wrapped in an old blanket, to the front room, where she announced the birth to my waiting grandmother: "Another girl!"

The fifth child and fourth girl of a pig-farming family, I was quite a disappointment to my widowed grandmother. She had hoped for many grandsons from her only son. Traditionally, the Chinese believe that "girls are losers," that the family brings up a girl only to lose her to the family that she marries into. Even though my parents were disappointed, they delighted in having a healthy new baby, boy or girl, especially since they had lost a newborn daughter the year before.

Our village of Pokfulam resembled an old Chinese village: small, dark houses built close to each other, separated only by unpaved narrow lanes. There was no running water, electricity or indoor plumbing; open sewage ran down both sides of the lanes. Most houses had thatched roofs and mud walls, some had dirt floors as well. In the rare brick house, a courtyard occupied the center, letting sunlight into the surrounding small rooms. Women did their cooking on wood-burning stoves in the courtyard or in the lane outside the house. Daily life was much like that lived in China centuries ago.

By 1929, China and the tiny British colony of Hong Kong were experiencing unprecedented cultural changes, greater than those of any previous dynastic upheaval. War, new technology, and availability of modern transportation and communication systems hastened these changes. Western ideas began to influence Chinese thinking. Feudal value systems became old-fashioned and impracticable. Governments changed. Rulers reformed. Revolutions occurred.

As my family thrived during this remarkable transition, my life and my education spanned the period and mirrored the times.

In childhood, I dutifully learned the three obediences — when at home, obey your parents; when married, obey your husband; when old, obey your son. The four feminine virtues

— beauty, honor, deportment and handicraft — were indelibly instilled in all women. My early education, however, was that of a nineteenth-century, feudal-society male scholar, studying the classics like someone who was preparing to take the Imperial Examinations. My values were solidly Confucian.

The Second World War displaced me from my comfortable home and I joined China's struggle for survival. Continuing my education in modern China, I learned a totally new set of values. Exposed for the first time to Christianity, I learned about religious faith. Preached to daily on the greatness of the Chinese people and the beauty of China, as well as on the importance of her winning the Second World War, I was unmistakably indoctrinated with nationalism.

When I was given the opportunity for advanced education across the sea, I came to a land with a new language and new beliefs, a land that gives everyone the right to "life, liberty and the pursuit of happiness." I studied advanced science and saw its benefits to mankind. I personally experienced democracy, independence and individual freedom; I also witnessed the triumph of the human spirit.

I have treasured these experiences and learned the importance of change and adaptation to the art of living. But all of this started in the little village of Pokfulam in Hong Kong.

The Love of Lotus

· 1 ·

Grandfather Wu

*A*round noontime, farmers stopped their work in the fields and gathered in the shade under nearby trees to rest and enjoy the lunches brought by their women folk. All was quiet except for the sound of their conversation, laughter and an occasional birdcall in the fields. In front of the farmers spread acres of rice paddies, filled with water, verdant with young plants. The narrow yellow paths separating the fields stood empty in the bright sun with only a few trees guarding the black, flooded soil and the small green plants.

Situated in southern China in the Pearl River Delta, the county of Far Yuen was blessed with rich soil and plenty of water. Located on the Tropic of Cancer, the region had a temperate climate — mild winters and warm summers. Farmers kept busy year round, some gathering three rice harvests a year. In villages throughout the county, peasants built houses in small clusters on high ground against the hill, each dwelling with a large patio in front facing the rice fields. In the spring, the red-tiled roofs and dark green brick walls of these houses contrasted with the green fields to present a colorful picture. Between production of abundant farm products and trade with neighboring areas, Far Yuen prospered for many centuries.

My grandfather, Wu Seh Sung, was born and grew up in the small village of Ta Dong Po in beautiful Far Yuen county. By the time he was born in the late 1800's, however, war had come to disrupt this idyllic region. The Qing Dynasty, after ruling China for over three hundred years, was in decline.

The imperial campaign to put down the Taiping Rebellion, from 1850 to 1864, drained the country's resources further. The leader of this Rebellion, Hung Hsiu-chuan, was a native son of Far Yuen County. Fierce fighting occurred in Far Yuen and spread as far north as Nanking. It took the Manchus more than a decade to defeat him.

By then Far Yuen was devastated; the economy did not recover for generations. As war raged and population grew, life in Far Yuen became a struggle, and men began leaving the area. Seh Sung and his wife were among the new immigrants to the British Colony of Hong Kong.

Like so many immigrants from China, they settled in an outlying village and made their livelihood in familiar trades such as growing vegetables, fishing, raising chickens and pigs. By supplying the growing city of Hong Kong with produce, meat and fresh seafood, these immigrants made a fairly good living for their families.

Seh Sung farmed pigs and eventually built a house for his family in the village of Pokfulam. From all accounts, Seh Sung was a stern, hardworking man with two daughters and a son. His daughters married young, one to a man working as steward in an ocean liner, the other to a well-to-do family in Pokfulam. He sent his son, Chung (but not his daughters) to Chinese school to study the classics for a few years then switched him to government schools to learn English — a rare concession to colonial rule. But soon work at the farm demanded that Chung stop attending school and help with the chores.

According to tradition, Seh Sung needed to arrange for his son's marriage when Chung became sixteen. A traditional man,

Seh Sung firmly believed his son should marry a woman from his own village or county, who would speak the same dialect and therefore would be more likely to have the Confucian virtues he valued. Chung would be obedient and marry the woman his father chose and they would have many sons to carry on the family name so Seh Sung could fulfill his most important duty to his ancestors.

On a sunny spring morning in Far Yuen County, in the hamlet of Cheak San Ghan (Foot of Mt. Elephant), a kiln-owner's family was busy preparing to receive an important visitor from Hong Kong. The head of this family was Kong Sahp-Sook, called Tenth Uncle Kong by most villagers because he was the tenth child in his family. Tenth Uncle had three daughters — aged sixteen, fifteen and thirteen — and two younger sons. He had recently contacted the village marriage broker and asked if she could find each daughter a good family into which to marry. Since Tenth Uncle owned a kiln and was quite prosperous and respected in the village, the marriage broker worked hard at her task. It was important for the families to be of the same social and economic stature, according to the principal of finding a "bamboo door to match a bamboo door, a wooden door to match a wooden door." After searching their small hamlet in vain, she went to the next village, where she heard that Seh Sung had come back from Hong Kong to look for a wife for his teenage son. This morning she was bringing him to talk to Tenth Uncle about his daughters and was hoping to start the marriage negotiations for these two families.

In Tenth Uncle's spacious living room, tea was served. The matchmaker, having already briefed the two men on family backgrounds, introduced them. They cordially greeted each other.

"It is kind of you to come all the way from Hong Kong to visit our humble house. We are much honored."

"Please don't mention it. It is indeed my honor to be able to make your acquaintance."

They discussed the state of affairs in Hong Kong and Far Yuen. Then it was time for Tenth Uncle to introduce his family. He called for them to come from the back parlor. First his wife, a small woman who managed a slight smile and sat quietly beside him. Then the eldest daughter, who was quite embarrassed to be introduced and stood awkwardly with her head lowered. The second daughter appeared. Standing straight, she politely acknowledged the guests as her father asked and smiled brightly. Her intelligent and sparkling eyes and her fine features caught Seh Sung's attention immediately, and he took an instant liking to the young lady. Third daughter, a shy, tiny girl, came out and turned her face to the wall. The two younger sons were healthy youngsters struggling to stand still. After a brief exchange of introductions, Tenth Uncle excused them. One by one, the five children of Tenth Uncle and his wife returned to the back room.

As required, Seh Sung bestowed many praises on the handsome family and expressed, indeed, his desire to become in-laws with Tenth Uncle. According to custom, the first to be married should be the eldest daughter. But Seh Sung asked if Tenth Uncle would mind letting his second daughter be his daughter-in-law. Tenth Uncle agreed to discuss the matter with his wife and let the matchmaker know. They parted amicably, agreeing to let the matchmaker arrange the details.

Word came the next day that Tenth Uncle and his wife agreed to let his second daughter, Sum, be married to Seh Sung's only son. The matchmaker noted the date and time of the girl's birth, and would take the young couple's birth dates and zodiac signs to the fortune teller to determine if they were compatible.

Even though the girl's strong zodiac sign indicated that she could bring harm to her husband, the fortune teller decided that the boy's signs, equally strong, were enough to withstand her. After the matchmaker checked back three generations to clear both sides for inheritable diseases such as leprosy or madness , everyone decided that it was a good match. The details of the marriage — such as how many roasted pigs and pieces of jewelry would be sent to the bride's family and how much "body's worth" (Sun Ka Money) should be sent by the groom's family — would be worked out through the matchmaker.

Seh Sung went back to Hong Kong and told his son Chung about the match. The young couple had not yet met each other, but Seh Sung was sure he had made the right choice for a daughter-in-law — after all, she came from a good family and grew up in the same county. Marriage was a matter to be arranged by parents, not by the young people themselves. The elders knew what would work in a marriage according to family background and circumstance. The custom had functioned for centuries.

My parents were married in December, 1919, obeying both sets of parents and without first meeting each other. (Actually, my father did go back to Far Yuen once to steal a surreptitious look at his bride-to-be.) My mother, at fifteen, thus began her life in Hong Kong, living with a stranger in a strange place with no family or friends nearby. Years passed before she had a chance to see her parents again.

The next year, Seh Sung's first grandson, Yingjim, was born, fulfilling the grandfather's obligation to his ancestors by having an heir to the family name. Seh Sung passed away a short time later, at a very young age. However, he died comforted by the knowledge that his family name would be carried on, thus his most important filial duty had been done according to Confucian teachings.

My father, Wu Chung, at the age of eighteen, became head of household with a young wife, a son, and a widowed mother. He worked dutifully at the farm with his family but was not happy with that kind of work. "Kneeling to feed the swine," as he put it, was humiliating to him. Even though he was making a good living for his family, he longed to try his hand at other, better trades.

When the farm sold a large litter of piglets and netted extra cash one year, my father suggested that he should use it for lessons to drive a taxicab so he could start a new career. His widowed mother objected: "Driving a car is a dangerous profession. You shouldn't do it." But both my parents saw that the newly introduced automobile provided a good method of transportation in the growing city of Hong Kong, and were convinced that there was future in the taxicab business. My father went ahead and became a taxicab driver. He left his family in Pokfulam and stayed in the city, working both day and night shifts. Within a short time, he was able to share ownership in a taxicab with a friend, a sikh. He became the sole owner after the friend decided to return to India and sold him the half share. Even though my father was not able to pay the full amount, the friend entrusted him with the taxicab and told him to pay as he had money. Enterprising and hard-working, in a few years (in fact by the year I was born) my father had become the owner of a small taxicab company. My mother would go to the city to live with him to help with the company and leave the care of my three older siblings — Yingjim, 9; Waijin, 7; and Waifong, 5 — in Pokfulam in the care of my grandmother.

"I will take the baby to the city and nurse her myself," Mother told my grandmother. "It would be too much for you to care for her, too." So I was taken from the house where I was born, and was nursed by my mother on the third floor of a tenement house in the old section of Hong Kong on Wanchai Road, where my parents had their first flat. Two years later, younger brother Yingchou was born there.

Shortly thereafter, my father moved his whole family, including my grandmother, to a newly built, bigger flat near the waterfront on Jaffe Road. My parents continued to have children, because the Chinese believed children were assets to the family. After Yingchou, there was another girl, Waitong. Then followed the three boys: Yingsheung, Yingkwong and, in 1942, my youngest brother Yingbun. In the days before contraceptives, my mother did her wifely duties and kept having children. She had a total of eleven pregnancies, of which two children died in infancy and nine of her offspring survived to adulthood.

· 2 ·

Jaffe Road

Our flat on Jaffe Road in Hong Kong was the first place I remember as home. We must have moved there when I was three or four years old. I don't remember the move nor anyone talking about it. I only knew that this was a brand new place and my mother was very happy to live there. Since my father was an only son, his mother was living with us as tradition dictated. Even though we had maids to take care of us, my grandmother often baby-sat and played with us. I can still recall wonderful times with her there.

Our complex was on new landfill in the harbor in the Wanchai waterfront area. The buildings were three stories tall with stairs between each pair of adjoining buildings. As all the buildings were connected, the apartments had light only from the front and the back. However, we were able to rent a well-lighted apartment on the second floor of the first building in the row, so our home had light from three sides. The south side, fronting the street, had a row of glass windows separating the living room from a small balcony, from which one could look over into the street below. This was my favorite hiding place.

The apartment was not large, consisting of only three bedrooms, a living/dining room, and a bathroom, with the kitchen connected to the main area by a narrow covered corridor. Kitchens were built away from the living area in those days for safety reasons. From the bedroom windows at the back, we could look across the harbor to Kowloon Peninsula and see the clock tower of the train station. During the typhoon season, balls were displayed on both sides of a pole atop the tower to signal the danger level of an approaching storm: a mild typhoon would rate two balls, a more serious one perhaps seven or eight.

The Hong Kong harbor was always busy. Shipping traffic, ocean liners and junks, pleasure craft and fishing boats plied the open water. In the afternoons and on weekends, I used to sit in front of the window watching them for hours on end, dreaming, wondering what was beyond the narrow window, the wide harbor, the ocean.

Next to our building across a narrow alley on the west side stood a police station, one of the main reasons my mother wanted to live there. She felt that a home next to a police station had to be safer than other places. From the moment I began to learn the way things worked, I understood that the city was full of dangers, one had to be protected, and policemen were there to protect us. Even though the police were much in evidence, we children were not allowed to go outside by ourselves, but had to have an adult with us even to go downstairs. We never played in the street for fear of through traffic and bogeymen lurking nearby. Remnants of this fear haunt me till this day.

Across the street from the police station was a large paved drill field, used by both the police and firemen. A tall steel tower stood on one corner, and firemen often ran up to the top of the tower to practice fighting fire. Whenever the firemen began their drills, my brother Yingchou and I would beg Grandmother to take us to the drill field. It was great entertainment to watch the firemen carrying empty fire hoses as they raced up to the top. The tower seemed very, very high to us little children, although in reality it was probably only four or five stories. When the captain gave the signal, water started to come out forcefully from the hoses they carried, and the firemen struggled to hold them tight to direct the jet of water onto a designated object on the ground. Once they set fire to a small wooden house on the ground for practice and we excitedly clapped and jumped with joy when the fire was put out.

On afternoons when the police or the firemen were not using the drill field, it became our playground. Grandmother would take us across the street and we played hide-and-seek or just chased each other, sometimes clambering up the steel stairs of the tower. We also jumped rope and played hopscotch. I remember many skinned knees and assorted bumps and bruises. We had no balls, tricycles, bicycles or other toys that I remember. Kites were prohibited in our family. I was told of instances reported in the newspapers about children who took their kites up to the roof of their buildings to fly and carelessly followed them too closely, fell from the roof and died. My childhood was full of cautions and warnings.

My older brother and two older sisters had been going to school ever since I could remember. Brother Yingjim, nine years older than I, was the eldest and was always treated with respect and admiration. Confucian ethics demanded submission or obedience to one's elders, including older brothers and sisters. As males were much valued in this culture, Yingjim was allotted a higher place in the family than the girls, and he demanded absolute respect from his three younger sisters. He would openly called us "girlies" in a derogative way and could get away with it. As he was very smart and received good grades in school, we were told to emulate him. Among ourselves, we called him Brother King. He relished his standing in the family tremendously and lorded over us. I learned early that there were great advantages in being a male or being able to do things as well as a male. I never wanted to be like my sisters, I only wanted to be like Yingjim, good grades and all.

Children were expected to be quiet and obedient, seen but not heard — especially girls. Chinese children were not expected to be active or play all the time. We had no dolls nor doll houses and I never learned to ride a bicycle. Reading and studying were encouraged, not playing with dolls. If we ever jumped or ran around the house in joy or laughter, my parents would admonish us, asking why we were so loud and noisy.

I was the fourth consecutive girl born to my parents. They wanted a boy so badly that they first called me Dai Tigh which means "bring little brother." Sure enough, the next baby born to them was Yingchou, a boy, two years younger than I. He and I were closer to each other than to the other siblings. My parents dressed me like him in boys outfits and treated me as if I were a boy. They continued this practice until it was time for us to go to school. I have often wondered whether their attitude had anything to do with the fact that I grew up believing there was no difference in ability between men and women. I always felt that whatever my brothers could do, I could do also.

On summer weekends, my parents would put us all in a car to go to the beach in Deep Water Bay or Repulse Bay for playing in the sand or swimming. We would go in the early morning. Yingjim became a very good swimmer, but I never did learn to swim. Instead, I built castles in the sand and dug elaborate tunnels between them, laboring the whole time only to have them destroyed, either by my mischievous brothers or myself, before we left. Then when we got home, we would have to clean all the sand and salt water from our bodies. It was a big fuss.

My parents decided that I should wait to start school with younger brother Yingchou, so I never went to kindergarten but started first grade when I was seven years old. I was sent to a girls' elementary school with my older sisters, while Yingchou was sent to a boys' school where our eldest brother attended. Both schools were nearby, and both were typical private schools concentrating on teaching Chinese classics. The principal in my brother's school also had an enviable reputation as a strict disciplinarian. He could mold any wild child into a learned scholar during the years that child spent in his school. My eldest brother could cite example after example of his schoolmates who went through whole weeks of detention and finally learned to memorize the required pages of *The Analects*, one of the four books recording Confucius' teachings. He told how the principal used a long thin ruler to beat on the upturned palms of a six- or seven-year-old until they would cry out the commitment to memorize the lessons.

To alleviate these horrors associated with attending school, my parents prepared Yingchou with the protection and blessings of Confucius. By custom, a child, especially a male one, usually started schooling with a ritual called "kai-mong" — an opening of the mind whereby a child was presented before the portrait of Confucius. After kneeling and making offerings of fruits and incense, he was encouraged to ask for guidance and blessing, so that he would be able to become a revered scholar someday. This request was also made to the principal and teachers of the school. The offerings in this case, however, instead of fruits and incense, were substantial sums enclosed in red envelopes, a traditional way of giving money. With this opening of the mind ritual, our intellectual adventure began, learning at a young age the philosophies and ethics of ancient China.

By the time I started school, the Imperial Examinations given by the Qing Court to find qualified administrators were long gone, dispensed with the Manchu Dynasty in 1911. But the tradition of classical learning was still very much revered. My father, being a traditionalist, insisted that all his children acquire a classical education. Such schools still existed in Hong Kong, though they were beginning to be considered old-fashioned. The more forward-looking families were now sending their children to English-speaking government-sponsored schools where children learned English as well as the sciences. These children would also learn to write the simpler modern Chinese rather than the difficult classical Chinese.

In the traditional schools, the method of learning followed that of the scholars in Dynastic China preparing to take the Imperial Examinations. Scholars learned the classics and memorized all Confucius' teachings until they knew them so well that whatever the examination required, they could recite and answer fully. The curriculum did not include mathematics, physics, biology, chemistry or any of the modern sciences, because the ancient examination system did not include these subjects. Most of the learning involved ethics and human relations according to Confucius, methods of governance and control in society. From winners of these examinations the Imperial Court chose officials to rule China. Since the Court favored ruling the country with Confucius ethics, only those who followed Confucian teachings had a chance of being chosen.

Every morning, after we were washed and dressed (the maids combed my long hair into two pigtails) and had breakfast, we all walked to school together, accompanied by an adult. Lunches were brought to us from home in a layered tin box containing a hot meal with rice. At about three o'clock, when school was out, someone would come and take us home. We had fresh fruits for snacks but no sweets or soda drinks, only tea or juices. My mother was never there when we came home because she worked with my father during the day, but she always left orders with the maids to give us fruit. I fondly recall eating California Sunkist oranges and red Washington Delicious apples. More than half a century ago, the United States was already exporting fruit to Hong Kong.

After snacks, we relaxed. I often sat in the balcony and watched activities on the busy street below. Cars were going to and fro, vendors with pushcart or baskets balanced on ends of a bamboo pole upon their shoulders called out their wares. Knife sharpeners, vegetable sellers, candy and preserved-fruit hawkers paraded in front of my eyes. Occasionally, my grandmother would give us money to buy roasted chestnuts, our favorite snack. We called our order down to the peddler for one, two, or three portions, then we put the money in a basket with a rope tied to its handle and lowered it to the street below. The vendor exchanged the money for the chestnuts, and we pulled the basket up to retrieve our treat. It was great excitement — besides having our beloved roasted chestnuts, we had the fun of lowering the basket and retrieving it.

Our schools had no libraries, nor did the city. (The only library in Hong Kong at the time, donated to the English language Hong Kong University by a famous Chinese, was not open to the general public.) Instead of buying books, we rented them. An itinerant book renter came every other day and displayed his books in the stairwell downstairs at the entrance of our apartment. Accompanied by an adult, we could go down to examine the offerings, and perhaps rent a book or two. The charge was only pennies per book for two days. His collection was mostly comic books of poor quality, printed on rice paper and put together in flimsy old-fashioned thread bindings. These books often pictured old myths and legends about deeds accomplished by magical Shaolin School monks who could fly over mountains and withstand numerous assaults by men or weapons, or about persons born with special talent who could win any battle and overcome hardship — all wonderful flights of fancy that stimulated the young imagination. However, our parents soon found out that we were reading this unrealistic literature and forbade us to rent them. They claimed that such flights of fancy could lead young minds into believing that magical deeds could be achieved by anybody who tried. Occasionally, the news reported a seven or eight year old child jumping from a three-story balcony believing he could fly, or a ten-year-old disappearing into the mountains to train for magical skills. That ended our fanciful literary adventure. For extracurricular readings from then on we turned to newspapers and magazines subscribed by our parents or older siblings.

We were encouraged to make our own toys. For playing the game of jacks, Grandmother taught us how to sew small squares of cloth together and fill them with tiny red beans. We also played "kick the swallow," now known as "hocky-sock," using a toy made of several feathers tied to a one-inch stack of heavy paper, anchored by an ancient coin with a hole in the middle, much like the badminton shuttlecock. A player kicked the swallow high in the air with his instep and tried to kick it again before it hit the ground on its return. When a good rhythm was established, a skilled player could go on for a long time, kicking the swallow hundreds of times without interruption. The one who could kick the swallow most times without missing it was declared winner. At night, we made shadow plays resembling birds or horses on the wall with our hands and fingers. With a simple string, we played "cat's cradle" for hours. But most of the time, we studied and read.

We also fought amongst ourselves a great deal, mostly about sharing things. I often wanted to go with my older sisters whenever they went out, to movies or with friends. Most of the time, they would not take me and I would scream and insist on going. Sometimes they placated me with a bribe of candy or a book. Actually, I preferred that to the movies. When we fought or did not do as the maids wanted, such as bathing at the appointed time, they would threaten us with: "I will tell Madame about you." I never believed that they would, but complied anyway.

My parents came home for dinner around six o'clock. From the age of five, we children sat at the table with them. Nobody started dinner until my father sat down, Mother usually was busy doing something and was frequently late to the table, annoying Father. We seldom waited for her. No child could start until everyone at the table was acknowledged individually. "Grandma have dinner, Papa have dinner, Mama have dinner, elder brother have dinner, elder sister have dinner, second elder sister have dinner," and so on down the line. I remember when youngest brother, Yingbun, first sat at the table, he was told to go around acknowledging his elders. As a five-year-old could not speak too fast, the litany would take him a while. One day, half-way through dinner, Father heard him saying: "Third elder brother have dinner," and asked what was happening.

Yingbun replied: "I am the youngest and have to acknowledge everyone at the table. It takes a long time."

"Hurry and finish," Father said, "so you can start eating."

We all laughed, but the ritual continued as long as we were having dinner with Father and Mother.

Children did not talk at the table unless asked a question.

We sat and listened quietly to whatever was discussed during dinner. Father discouraged any unpleasant subjects including disciplinary topics. He preferred jokes or funny things that had happened during the day, believing these would help digestion. We greatly appreciated his decision. Any questions concerning discipline were usually dealt with after dinner.

After dinner, we started our homework. Each child would go to his favorite spot and start memorizing lessons aloud. The living room was the noisiest place, with at least two children studying there. Some of us finished quickly, but others took a long time. Third brother, Yingsheung, still remembers how, by overhearing younger sister Waitong, he was able to learn the poem that she was memorizing long before she did. We spent a couple of happy hours on our studies before we went to bed. Often we discussed the lessons together, with Yingjim explaining the subtitles. Before I went to bed, I would reorganize the the books and materials I needed for school in the rattan basket I took to school the next day, arranging them in the order needed on our schedule, making sure that I had everything ready, all the required homework done, ready to be handed in. By nine o'clock, most of us were in bed.

· 3 ·

Intellectual Adventure

*T*wo types of schools existed in Hong Kong in the 1930s: private schools for Chinese classics taught in the traditional way and public schools opened by the the British Government to teach English. The former used Chinese for instruction and the latter used English. In addition to reading and writing, the government schools taught mathematics and modern science, but the private schools did not have these subjects in the curriculum. Both were segregated schools. In our family, the boys attended the private Dungmei Boys Elementary School and the girls went to the private Jundak Girls Elementary School. After six years, we attended the government schools. This way, our education covered Chinese and English languages as well as both ancient and modern cultures.

Like my two older sisters, I started first grade in Jundak Girls Elementary. Every morning at eight o'clock, Waijin, Waifong, and I walked the mile or so up Wanchai Road to the ancient mansion that had been converted to our school. We climbed the ten wide impressive steps into the central hall where the grand stairs led up to my sisters' classrooms on the second floor. I went left to my first-grade room on the first floor to join my thirty classmates.

As soon as we saw each other, my classmates and I would start talking, shouting all at once, noisily telling each other all that had happened since we were last together. We could hardly wait to show our new pencils, book covers and anything else we had acquired overnight. If there were enough time, we would play a game of "picking up rocks," or "cat's cradle," with strings.

When a bell rang in the hall, we all ran to our assigned seats and waited. As the teacher entered, we stood and chanted in unison: "Good morning, Miss Song." Miss Song smiled and motioned us to sit down. The class routine was always the same.

"Let's start by reciting the lesson from yesterday," Miss Song said, "the Tang poem Saying Goodbye by Wong Wai." In sing-song rhythm, we recited together:

> Ha ma yum gwun tsao,
> Mun gwun haw saw tzee?
> Gwun yin bat dak tze,
> Gwai ngaw nam saan suey.
> Daan hoey mawk fook mun,
> Bak wun moh djun tsie.
> *(Getting off my horse and drinking with you,*
> *I ask, Where are you going?*
> *You reply, "My talents are not recognized.*
> *I am returning to the South Mountain to rest."*
> *Since you left, I have not heard.*
> *Only silent, white clouds forever filling the sky.)*

Miss Song then called on students to stand in front of the class and recite poems we had learned some days before. I remember one girl who could seldom recite as asked. One day, after several failed attempts, she was told to extend her right hand and Miss Song hit it hard with a ruler until the hand turned bright red.

"The pain will remind you to study hard," Miss Song said.

Without shedding a tear, the girl returned to her seat and sat down.

In the meantime, a classmate who would not stop talking in class was punished by being made to stand alone in front of the class until dismissal.

Most of the time, we followed Miss Song, reciting new poems out loud, in unison. These sing-song recitals went well with the rhymes. They helped me memorize the beautiful sounds of the poem, but I had no idea what the lines meant. I just memorized and recited as required.

After the lessons on Tang poems, we had calligraphy, a very important part of scholarly training. We would fill in the blanks in a copy book with Chinese brush and ink. It was hard for a youngster to hold the brush in the specific way, upright and straight in the right hand, the wrist flat yet not resting on the table. Using the left hand was not allowed even if you were naturally left-handed. Then came the difficult task of trying to fill in the narrow, intricate spaces that formed the characters.

"That is why you have to practice and practice," Miss Song told us. "Some day you should be able to do them all without the copy book." A Chinese scholar not only had to know classics but also had to have beautiful handwriting. Otherwise, he or she might be mistaken for an illiterate!

Then we studied arithmetic. I enjoyed that subject and prided myself in memorizing the multiplication table and solving difficult problems.

After lunch, we had three more classes: ancient texts, geography and sewing. There were no music lessons, no gymnasium or athletics, no drawing or science.

During the first year, school held no meaning for me, made no intellectual impact. I just loved the company of my classmates. I did not understand why we were studying. At the end of the year, when I placed number eighteen in the first-grade class of thirty-one, my achievement did not meet my parents expectations. They demanded that hereafter, I must study hard like my elder brother Yingjim, the model for us all. Yingjim always placed in the top three in his class. I so wanted to achieve, to please my parents, and to be a "good girl." From then on, being a good student became my driving ambition.

In second grade, we had Miss Chuk, a bright, young teacher who patiently explained the lessons and made them interesting. One lesson she taught was the essay *Love of Lotus*. In classical Chinese, the author praised the lotus flower:

> growing out of the mud and not being sullied,
> cleansing itself in the clear water and not being proud.
> Its stems are hollow inside and straight outside,
> lofty and unbranching.

The significance of the words was totally lost on me. But Miss Chuk explained that the lotus plant was here viewed as if it had human characteristics. Besides its beauty, the lotus possessed virtues we should all emulate: not to be influenced by an unhealthy environment, not be tainted by the mud; to be straightforward, not devious or branching. Of course! That was why the piece had become a classic and why we were studying it — to help us build character.

As I listened to her explanations, the lessons began to have meaning, I understood what the authors intended, not just the nice-sounding words. I marveled at the use of such wonderful writings to delineate moral teaching and quickly developed a love for the language.

Tang poems were written in the form of five or seven words to a line with four or eight lines to a stanza or poem, all according to rules on straight meter and coupling. One had to be well acquainted with the language and drilled in the rhyme books for years in order to write these poems, which are often full of allusions and images. The following poem, for instance, has only scenery and sound.

> "Crowing of Roosters,
> Thatched roof inn,
> Moon.
> Footprints,
> Wooden bridge,
> Frost."

As one reads the poem, one imagines footprints on the frost of a wooden bridge, feeling the cold morning in the country-side near a thatched-roof inn, listening to roosters crow.

The ancient poets were expected to write poems depicting paintings, and the best painters were supposed to draw paintings like poems.

Talented scholars wrote about everything, from love of a woman to love for country, friends, and home. These themes became familiar to all Chinese schoolchildren. One of my favorite poems concerned a young man who left home:

> Having left home a young man,
> I returned aged.
> My accent had not changed,
> But my hair had turned gray.
> The children greeted me,
> Without recognition.
> Laughingly they asked,
> "Whence come you, honored guest?"

The image that some day I would go away and return with

my hair white was firmly imprinted in my young mind. I never asked why I should have to go away, only felt sad about it.

My admiration of these convoluted verses and arcane poems was unending. I learned the metaphors in every stanza, the symbolism in every verse, and the philosophical essence in each essay. I studied not only the texts, but also the footnotes, for that's where the nuances were found! To make sure I knew my lessons well, I habitually got up early to review them before school. I could often be found on the balcony of our flat at five or six o'clock in the morning, reciting loudly. Emboldened by the smell of the early morning air, so invigorating in its freshness, so quiet in the stillness before everyone was up, I happily sang the rhymed words into the silence.

We also memorized the classical Four Books of Confucian philosophy: *The Great Learning*, *The Doctrine of the Mean*, *The Analects* and *Mencius*. The Master said: "To be able to learn and review what you studied frequently, is it not happiness? To have friends visiting from afar, is it not a delight? To be not angry even when one's talent is not recognized, is it not gentlemanly?" To be gentlemanly, or to be a "guantze," was to be an honorable, courteous, courtly, dependable, well-educated and dignified individual. That was the ultimate goal of a Confucian scholar. It was indelibly imprinted in my mind. I can still recite these writings from memory, page after page in that sing-song manner, as I did every day for my teacher.

Like a good Confucian scholar, I followed these teachings. These were moral codes and philosophies, not religious doctrines. Confucius prescribed exacting self-discipline, harmonious human relations and sensible state craft but never mentioned a supreme being except Heaven. Nor did he discuss life after death, saying: "Not knowing about life, how could one know about death?" His moral codes, not his religion, ruled China for over two thousand years.

On self-discipline, he said, "I examine my life daily with three criteria: "Did I work honestly for others? Was I faithful to my friends? Did I review what was taught me?" These were rules I lived by. My world was much like that of an ancient scholar. I fancied myself a talented Li Chingchao, a lady scholar in the Sung Dynasty. Someday, I would take the Imperial Examinations. I had to excel so that I could serve the Emperor. Confucius described the five human relations, "Wu Lun," as between "Emperor and subjects, father and son, brothers, husband and wife, and friends." The prescribed modes of behavior for these relations were: "loyalty, filial piety, kindness, fidelity, and trustworthiness," in that order.

My goals and ideals in life were to "discipline myself, unify the family, govern the country, and pacify the world," as the code of conduct for a Confucian scholar demanded.

At the age of eight, I memorized the principles of governance: "To rule with virtue is to prosper, to rule with force is to be a tyrant." When I become Governor, I vowed I should rule with virtue, not by force.

My siblings and I often challenged each other to recite these poems and ancient writings. On an outing or at home, my father would start by reciting one sentence and the rest of us immediately followed with the next sentence. We went on and on, as though singing beautiful songs with luscious verses that stirred our emotions. I can still feel the camaraderie and joy of these occasions. The last time I visited my father in Hong Kong before he passed away at the age of ninety, we spent our afternoons reciting classics together. When I stumbled, he chided me for "giving back my learning to my teacher." His memory had not failed him in the least. Even with his limited schooling of only a few years, he had memorized these classics for a lifetime.

In school, the five or six brightest girls played a game of Emperor and his court. We designated the brightest student as Emperor of the Chou Dynasty, while the rest of us became his ministers or his concubines playing at our imagined roles. Sometimes I played the most royal prime minister, advising his Majesty on grave subjects such as whether to invade the neighboring kingdom. At other times, I played a discarded concubine, dying of heartbreak and neglect. We all became immersed in the world we were studying.

We did not study science, not even a combined chemistry/ biology class. I knew nothing of the scientific method of investigation nor of the workings of chemistry and the human body until I was in high school and college. I cannot say that at the time I missed taking these subjects.

In history classes, we memorized the Chinese dynasties: Xia, Shang, Chou, Qin, Han, Jin, Shui, Tang, Song, Yuan, Ming, Qing, and the Republic. We learned each dynastic cycle, how the last descendent of the dynastic founder, in some cases more than three hundred years later, became complacent, corrupt and uncaring. The inept ruler was inevitably overthrown and a new dynasty was founded. The details were different, and we had to know them, but the lesson was always the same: one could rule only if one had the Mandate of Heaven. Moral fortitude and compassion for the populace were prerequisites for receiving the Mandate of Heaven. There were no exceptions. Ruling emperors were deposed whenever they lost the Mandate of Heaven.

I rejoiced in the study of the classics for the beauty of their use of language, their intricate polemics and philosophies and their promises of glory. I was told that in the classics one would find "golden houses and ravishing beauties." I believed that if I was good enough to be the top scholar in the imperial examination, I would be honored by the authorities.

The classics described a harmonious world in which there was order, everyone knew his or her place and individual duties were clearly defined. And in case of conflict, and history repeatedly showed there were conflicts, there would be proven methods of resolution. It was a kind, gentle, traditional and well regulated world. One only needed to follow the rules and principles of Confucius: everything would be fine. There was the benevolent emperor. He would rule justly, always.

As we studied the last dynasty, Qing, I found out that the Emperor was overthrown and had been replaced by a president in 1911. We were told that China had entered an age in which republican democracy, not imperial rule, would be the form of government.

Nothing in the classics explained what democracy was or how it would work. We were always subjects of the emperor, obeying his orders. In colonial Hong Kong, no one was talking or learning about democracy. I had no idea how I would fit into the World of Democracy. I knew only that there would no longer be Imperial Examinations and no more Emperors for me to serve. I was at a loss as to how, when I grew up, I could apply all my classical learning to help govern China.

I had no concept of the social and political convulsions that China was going through.

· 4 ·

Good Grades

*A*s soon as the bell rang, I ran out of our classroom, through the hall to the front door, down the wide steps onto the street. My two sisters were there waiting for me as usual. We turned left and walked the one hundred yards to the street corner toward our restaurant. My Second Elder Sister held my hand and cautioned me to be careful as we crossed the tram rails on Hennessy Road. In no time we were standing in front of the counter at our favorite cafe asking to be seated.

"I will have noodle soup with wonton."

"I'll have beef fried noodles."

"In that case, I'll have fried rice. Tea for all of us please."

It was the end of the school year and my sisters had grades on their minds. "We are going to be given report cards this afternoon. I am not going to worry about it. Miss Yen is so unfair. She always gives her favorites good grades and I never have a chance. I hate her," Eldest sister Waijin said.

"I wish I were a favorite of somebody," I whispered.

"So what if one is top three in class. I will never be the top student anyway. Fungjun is so smart, she will be number one always." Second Elder Sister Waifong said.

"I was number eighteen last year, I will be that again," I chimed in.

"It is not ordained, you know. How can you be so sure? Besides, with you second-graders, who cares? Only with us sixth graders are report cards important. We have to go to junior high next year, you know."

"I don't want to think about that even though I still have another year to go. So let's just forget it," Waifong said.

It was a good lunch; I ate the whole plateful of fried noodles. Afterwards Eldest Sister Waijin paid the bill and bought us preserved fruits and candies for a snack. We went back to school just in time for the afternoon classes.

After the last period, sewing, Miss Goh, our principal, brought us the report cards. As soon as she walked in we all stood and chanted in unison: "Good afternoon, Miss Goh."

She called each of us by name to go to the front. As she handed us the report card, she made some comments.

"Waiying, you did well this year. Continue the good work." Miss Goh put her hand on my shoulder as she gave me my report card. I noticed that some girls in my class were looking at me with a smile as I walked back to my seat.

"That was an unusual gesture. Did that mean that I would be her favorite now ? I will ask Second Elder Sister about that," I thought to myself.

My two sisters met me at the front steps after school and we began the familiar mile walk home. Turning right down the hill on Wanchai Road, we came to the intersection at Hak Street. Again, turning right down this short street, we crossed Hennessy Road to Stewart Road. There, one block past Lockhard Road, would be our home on Jaffe Road.

My two sisters were arguing loudly. Waifong wanted to talk about Miss Yen and how well she taught her Tang poetry class. Waijin thought all that was of "no-use."

"I want to see Lana Turner in that new film tomorrow. She is so beautiful! It is playing at the Tung Fong Theater now. I am sure we can go to the two-thirty after catching the noon show of Clark Gable at the Grand. We will ask Grandma to come with us."

"I want to go to Fungjun's house to play basket ball in Happy Valley this weekend. They have invited me. We so seldom get invited to any body's house. I hope Mama will let me go."

"She won't let you. You shouldn't play ball anyway. That's for boys. You will get all dark from sunburn and you will become a tomboy. Mama won't let you."

"Glamorous stars and movies, that's all you are interested in. I bet Mama won't let you go to the movies either."

"Hey, Waiying, where are you going? We turn right here." Waifong shouted at me as I absentmindedly kept walking straight on Wanchai Road. She grabbed my arm and we turned down Hak Street together.

I wanted to ask my sisters about Miss Goh and how could anyone become her favorite, but they kept arguing.

There were fresh oranges and apples waiting on the dining table at home. I let go of my rattan basket carrying the heavy books and dived in. That was the treat of the day. The maids always had fruits for us when we got home. Mama had given orders for that in the morning before she left with Baba to work.

Afterwards, I looked for books, magazines and newspapers to read. That year, by the end of my second grade, I was able to read newspapers and magazines. My sisters had subscribed to a weekly children's magazine, *Sister Yun,* for us. When it arrived, we all fought to read it first, and I was usually the last one to get it. The magazine articles were well written and accompanied by beautiful colored pictures. There were puzzles, riddles and stories written for seven to seventeen year-olds. It was the first book or magazine, besides the newspapers, written in modern Chinese that I read. I could read it without translation, unlike the classical textbooks we studied. It was delightful to read something simple, to the point and about everyday life, not written in ancient classical language like what we studied in school.

During these hours, I usually immersed myself in my own little hemisphere reading about the world at large, about the struggle in China, catching up with life. My sisters and brothers would each do things they liked. Occasionally, Grandma would take us little kids to play across the street in the large concrete paved drill field. In the crowded city this was a convenient place for us to throw a ball, play hide and seek or just run around. We loved to climb up the tower where firemen practiced. The tower served as our Jungle Gym.

Mama and Baba came home at six o'clock. We all gathered for dinner at the table.

"How was school?"

"We got our report cards today!"

"We will take a look at them after dinner," Baba said. He never liked to have serious conversations during dinner, for fear it would interfere with the pleasure of the meal.

At dinner, I noticed that Waifong, our second elder sister, was served a big steamed chicken leg on a separate dish all for her. It must be her birthday, I thought. In our house, birthdays for children were not celebrated nor even mentioned, as the Chinese custom dictated, for fear that the gods would hear and "snatch" the child away. The children knew only when they were served with extra delicious food for dinner. A Chinese starts to celebrate his birthday when he reaches sixty or seventy years old. By then, he can assume that the gods would no longer be jealous of him would leave him alone; then he might toast and celebrate his life a little.

After dinner, we all went to our rattan baskets for our

report cards. I was filled with anxiety, not knowing what to expect.

We all stood by Baba's chair. Mama was sitting at his right hand side, not smiling. She had that severe and judging expression on her face. I was always afraid to look at her when she was like that, afraid that she would become angry and start to scold me for something or other. I looked down at my feet.

Eldest sister Waijin handed Baba the report card when he asked for it.

"Number thirty two! Last one again!" Baba exploded. "What are we going to do with you? You are so lazy. You just want to be pretty and glamorous, you won't study. Nothing will ever become of you!"

Eldest sister Waijin just stood there stony faced, not saying a word. My mother looked at her in disgust and said: "You are USELESS!"

Then it was second elder sister Waifong's turn. Baba looked at the report card and sighed. "When are you going to do better than number fifteen? I know you work hard, but number fifteen will not do. You should be like your older brother. He is number one in his class all the time. You think you can do better next year?"

"Yes, Baba. I will try," Waifong mumbled with a bowed head.

"All right, Waiying, let's see how you are doing this year."

I handed Baba my report card quietly.

"So you are third in your class this year! Top three, that's pretty good. Much better than last year's eighteenth!" I heard Baba comment.

"Good girl!" Mama was so excited, she jumped out of her chair, grabbed and hugged me. I was totally surprised, for I could not remember ever being hugged by her before. It is most unusual in a Chinese family for parents and children to get physically close like that. I did not know how to react. I just stood there stiffly with my hands hanging down at my side and waited awkwardly. Mama had her arms and whole body wrapped around me, and she practically lifted me up. Finally she let me go and said: "Of course, you can always improve. Next year, maybe you will be first in your class. All right? Just study hard."

I could see the pride in her eyes. She had always told us to be like Eldest Brother Yingjim, to be the first in our class. But I had no idea what that meant. I only knew she favored him terribly. Maybe it was because he was her first born, the eldest son in the family, I thought. But now I could sense the same softness in her voice she used when she spoke to him. Mama favored Yingjim because he made good grades! If I had good grades, perhaps she would favor me too!

"You two should be like Waiying. She is a good and obedient girl." She instructed my two older sisters.

Mama actually told my older sisters to be like me! Imagine that!

Mama finally had noticed me. She even had hugged me! All I had to do was to study hard, which I loved anyway. I knew how to do it, I knew the way to have Mama love me! I knew!

Even though I never had a chance to ask Waifong if Miss Goh in school will treat me as her favorite pupil from now on, I went to bed happy and content that night, secure in the knowledge that to be loved by Mama, all I had to do was just study hard and be top three in my class. I could do that! I knew how.

· 5 ·

New Horizons

*T*he May Fourth Movement in 1919 occurred after the founding of the Republic. It was begun by students in Beijing to protest mistreatment of China by foreign countries after the First World War. The movement eventually centered on education and language reform. Instead of using classical Chinese, the students demanded that an easier, plain-speaking language, the dialect spoken in Beijing, be used in writing instead of the difficult classical prose. They insisted that schools should teach this new form of writing as well as modern subjects such as science — not just the dead classics, which were used only by the Mandarins or scholars. They realized that China had to find an easier way to educate its people, to catch up with the rest of the world.

By the time I could read in the mid-1930s, literary magazines, newspapers, children's books, and translations of foreign literature were all in plain language. These publications emphasized new ideas, not the craftsmanship of the language, and introduced new Western ideals such as individualism and democracy. I was totally captured by the concepts and had no trouble understanding the simpler texts. In school, however, I still studied and wrote in classical Chinese and did not write plain language until I was in high school. My elder brother, Yingjim, continued to write in classical Chinese his entire life.

In addition to serialized novels and stories published in

newspapers, I also encountered modern literature in a children's weekly magazine published by someone with the pen name "Elder Sister Yun." My sisters subscribed to this publication, and every week I eagerly awaited its arrival. Happily I turned its pages to look at the bright photos of young children at play, to connect the numbered dots to find the animal of the week, to color pictures to find out what stories they told, and, of course, to read new and exciting tales about children in China and the rest of the world.

In time, I started reading literature discussed or recommended in the magazine: writings of Lu Xun, Ba Gin, Ding Ling, and others who vividly described life in modern China.

The most famous of these writers was Lu Xun, who wrote with exacting and barbed prose, compassionate insight and satiric precision about the ignorance, selfishness, and sufferings of the Chinese people. His attack on government corruption was legendary, as well as was his indictment of the complacency of the people. His famous satire, *The True Story of Ah Q*, described a young illiterate peasant who went to his execution without really understanding why he was to die at the hands of a firing squad. Yet Ah Q thoroughly enjoyed the attention accorded him in the parade through the streets of his little town, as tradition would have it, before he was executed. As he walked up to the platform and was positioned to be shot, he felt compelled to give a show for the onlookers, perhaps even sing a few operatic arias. But in his confusion, he could only shout at the crowd triumphantly: "After twenty years, I will be another good man."

The phrase "the spirit of Ah Q" has since become a popular metaphor for self-deception.

Lu Xun became my literary and political hero. His plaintive cry, "save the children," at the end of his famous short story

"The Diary of a Madman" established him as the conscience of modern China. His essay "Roads Were Forged by People Treading on Them" was the guidepost for brave young Chinese then and still is. He originally went to Japan to study medicine so he could save lives and alleviate suffering. However, after watching a Japanese newsreel showing Manchurian Chinese cheering at a Japanese execution of Chinese peasants during the Russo-Japanese War, he decided it was more important to save the souls of the Chinese people than their lives, and went back to Beijing to teach and write. I vowed, in 1938 when I was nine years old, that someday I too would become a Lu Xun to wake up the country with my writings so China would be saved from ignorance, selfishness, and apathy.

Ba Gin, a writer of epic novels concerning the Chinese family, was another of my heroes. His best known novel, *Home,* described the struggles within a traditional family where five generations lived in the same compound, governed first by an aged grandfather and later, after the grandfather died, by an inept and weak eldest son. Ba Gin defined the Chinese pictograph, home, as "swine under the gilded roof." In episode after episode, he depicted conflicts between the filial piety demanded by Confucius and the new ideas of freedom and individual rights. He portrayed young lives repeatedly and tragically sacrificed for ancient moral codes simply because the young were supposed to obey their elders. These books made deep impressions on my young mind. I began to question the wisdom of ancient moral codes.

I was also introduced to nineteenth-century Russian and world literature. The Chinese society of the early 1900s was similar to that of Czarist Russia. Poor Chinese peasants and Russian serfs suffered the same starvation, misery, and deprivation. The fruits of their labor were enjoyed solely and unashamedly by the privileged. Excellent translations of novels by Dostoyevsky, Tolstoy, and Turgenev were widely published and circulated. These wonderful novels opened up a fascinating world for me.

At the age of ten, I was reading *Anna Karenina* and *Jean Christopher*. I sobbed for Anna when she threw herself under the train. I felt the burden of the future as I read the last paragraph of *Jean Christopher*, when St. Christopher arduously carries the child across the river and asks: "Child, who art thou?" and the child answers: "I am the days to come." Many of these images remain with me to this day.

I also read Shakespeare's plays in Chinese translation. For many years, I wondered why he was regarded as one of the great playwrights, for, personally, I preferred Russia's Chekhov or Norway's Henrik Ibsen. Not until years later, when I could read Shakespeare in English, did I begin to appreciate his talents in the use of language. Just as those people who read Tang poems in English or other languages may not fully understand and appreciate their beauty, I was unable to enjoy Shakespeare's craftsmanship in translation.

From these great novels and plays I vicariously experienced human aspirations, compassion, and a wide range of other emotions. I learned as well the romantic notions of love, the idea of *noblesse oblige*, and the ultimate value of human freedom. These thoughts and beliefs gradually grew in my mind as my physical and temporal world changed. My eclectic readings saved me from becoming a dogmatic Confucian, following the ancient doctrines to the letter and devoting unyielding loyalty to the ruler and filial piety to parents. The humanistic ideals enlightened and freed me, enabling me to appreciate twentieth-century values, especially individualism and human freedom.

Of all the rules Confucians followed, the most important was obedience. One was to obey the authorities, one's superiors, one's elders, and first of all, one's parents. This principle of obedience was used to rule China for centuries, and the emperor was able to keep the submissive society peaceful and prosperous for long periods of time. Chinese civilization even flourished under it. These traditions kept Chinese society orderly without promulgating extensive legal regulations. Subjects of the emperor should simply obey, whatever his edicts — there was no need for legislation.

In our family, as in any Chinese family, obedience to parents was strictly enforced. We not only obeyed our parents, but our elders as well. Younger brothers and sisters were supposed to "listen" to their older brothers and sisters and not object to their "orders."

"Teng wah," or "listening," which meant following my elders' orders and wishes, was a strong and good point in my character. My mother always praised me for "listening" to her, acting according to her wishes. For my part, I cannot remember any hardship in following her advice and obeying her. Most of the time, she just wanted me to study hard and be a good girl. Since I did not find anything wrong with that, I was often the object of her praise and rewards after she decided that I was indeed obedient. I enjoyed these rewards and ample praises. It was gratifying, and I felt that I was really loved by her.

The Confucian ethics demanded that the subject who did not obey his emperor should be punished or put to death. Parents also had the power to punish or kill their children for disobedience depending on the seriousness of the offense. I had taken this to heart. Anyone who "disobeyed" was not only wrong, but perhaps did not even have the right to exist! Yet, I was learning about the importance of individuals, about freedom, and about an entirely new set of values. This changed my whole system of beliefs, leading to uncompromising conflicts and struggles that I would have to face for years.

· 6 ·

My Portrait

"*A*ren't they beautiful?" My cousin Ah Won asked the question as we picked up the proofs from the shop where we had had our portraits taken a week ago. We both had anxiously anticipated the outcome of these pictures for the whole long week. It was the first time my cousin had ever had a portrait taken.

Ah Won was my maternal aunt's daughter. She had come from the village in China to live with us in Hong Kong. She was older than I, even older than my two older sisters. But I knew she was still quite young. She was not married and certainly not as old as my mother or grandmother.

We had a lot of fun together. She took me to school in the morning and brought me back home in the afternoon. For some reason, she did not go to school with me, just walked me there and back. My mother said she was here to take care of us, but she was not a maid, she was our cousin.

We played together, went shopping and to the movies. There was a standing order in our house that we little kids were not to go any place without the company of an adult. But with Ah Won I could go almost anywhere. During our walk to and from school, we talked a lot. She told me that she did not know how to read or write. I thought it curious because I had been to the elementary school for only three years and I could read Tang poems, newspapers, magazines, street signs and advertisements without any difficulty. Surely, at her age, she had been to school for at least three years and had learned to read.

"You don't know. In the village, they don't teach girls to read. Only boys get to go to school."

"Girls are human too! You can go to school with us, our school is a girls' school. It teaches us girls to read."

"But you're only ten. I am already fifteen, I am too old to go to school now."

I did not know the customs in the village, but I did know that there was no girl in my class as old as fifteen. Maybe Ah Won did not need to learn to read after all.

A week ago, on Friday, we passed by a photograph shop on Hennessy Road on our way back from school. I was reading aloud a sign posted in front of the store that said: "Portraits, a dollar a person with three different poses." We stopped to look at the samples on display.

Ah Won said, "That is very reasonable and they are good portraits. Shall we try it?"

"That should be fun! Why not?"

"I have never had a portrait taken. Maybe I can send one back to my Mom in the village."

So we went inside and had our portraits taken, three different poses for each of us. In no time, it was done. Ah Won paid the total cost of two dollars.

"For both of us," she said, "because you are the one who found this bargain!"

A week later, the photograph shop gave us the untouched proofs and informed us that if we wanted any of the portraits retouched and printed, it would cost a dollar apiece.

We looked at these untouched images of ourselves proudly. Ah Won, with her short hair which she started to wear after she came to live with us, looked radiant with her shy smile in one pose. I, with two long pigtails, one on each side of my face, wearing my school uniform, though not smiling, looked fetching in one of my poses. Two happy and healthy young girls were captured in a special moment.

We were satisfied and did not spend the money to have them retouched.

When we got home, we happily showed them to my grandmother. She thought they were good likenesses of both of us. "Pretty girls," she said.

We could hardly wait to show them to my parents after dinner, hoping they would give us the money to have one or two portraits printed, perhaps even one enlarged to hang on the wall. Ah Won could send one to her mother.

After dinner, I handed my mother the proofs. "Mama, Ah Won and I had some portraits taken last week and we have the proofs today. Here they are. Which one do you like best?"

My mother looked at them carefully one by one but did not say anything. Finally, when she spoke, she sounded angry. Ah Won and I just stood there, looking very uncomfortable, unable to explain anything.

"So you dare to do something like this by yourself. Who gave you permission to do a big deal like this? You, you daring, disobedient child," my mother yelled at me.

"Ah Won and I did it together, Mama. We both had our portraits taken."

"That's no excuse. You should have asked for permission first. How dare you to decide to do that on your own? You must be itching for Baba to give you a beating! Get me the feather duster."

Before I realize what was going on, I was yanked in front of Baba and he started to beat me with the feather duster.

"Why didn't you ask for permission before you did it? You know you should not make such big decisions by yourself."

"Baba, I didn't know . . . !" I cried as I jumped around to avoid the feather duster bearing down on me.

"She is just a child, spare her," Grandmother pleaded with her son.

"You keep out of this, Nana. You always interfere when we discipline the children. Children should be taught important lessons, otherwise, they go wild!" Mama tried to quiet her mother-in-law.

"Ah . . . Ah, it hurts. I hurt, I hurt . . . I"

"Just on the legs, not her body or face." Mama yelled to Baba while I tried to avoid the feather duster.

"If you want to beat . . . beat me, not her," Grandmother shouted as she thrust herself at Baba in a struggle to rescue me.

While Grandmother interfered with Baba, I quickly escaped into the bathroom at the far end of the house and locked the door. There, no one can get at me. I sat on the toilet seat cover examining the bloody marks on my legs and started to howl louder and louder. The pain in my legs is palpable, but I could stop the bleeding and make the wounds heal. It was the hurt to my pride that was unconsolable. What did I do wrong? Why are they beating me for having my portrait taken? Why do my parents want me to ask for permission to do that? Must I ask permission for doing everything, for living? For what reasons must I ask? Mama always said that I should be obedient, do as I was told.

She wanted to control me completely . . .

After a while, as I began to calm down, I heard grandmother's soft voice outside the bathroom:

"Don't cry. Let me come in to clean you up."

I remembered that she had given me comfort from a

beating once before. Grandmother did not approve of Mama's way of dealing with us. She told me that when Baba was beating us, she felt as if he was beating her. It hurt her even more than it did us.

I opened the door slowly and buried my face in Grandmother's arms.

· 7 ·

War Comes

December 8, 1941, was a Monday in Hong Kong, and our household went about its usual morning activities. Eldest brother Yingjim was already up and dressed in his white shirt and blue school jacket with the insignia of the Hong Kong University on the left-hand pocket. He teased his two younger brothers, still in bed: "Come on, sleepyheads, time to get up."

I could hear my older sisters Waijin and Waifong arguing in their room: "You can't have my green pencil today. I need it for my drawing class."

"You promised I could have it for the week."

Younger sister Waitong was putting her school books in the rattan carrying basket. Yingkwong, too young to go to school, was still sound asleep in my Grandma's bed. My parents were already dressed for work, and the maids were setting the table.

I had an examination that day and was quite nervous about a lesson I had not memorized well. We had a tough teacher that year in the sixth grade, and I had been up since five that morning trying to prepare myself.

As we sat down to breakfast, second brother Yingchou rushed in with his right arm in one sleeve of his school jacket and his left arm groping for the other sleeve behind his back. My father smiled at him and said, "You are always late." Then the sirens started.

We had had intermittent air-raid drills for the past year because the Japanese were stepping up military activities in Southern China, so the piercing sound was familiar, even anticipated. The government always announced the drills in advance. But this siren was unexpected. As the sound wailed through the morning air, my parents turned on the radio.

In an unsteady voice, the radio announcer said that a group of Japanese planes had been sighted flying toward Hong Kong from the northeast. "This is an air-raid warning, not a drill. Repeat, not a drill." As we listened, we looked toward Kowloon from our home by the shore of Hong Kong Island. Columns of black smoke were rising into the sky. Kowloon had been bombed! The radio reported that the Japanese had bombed Singapore and Pearl Harbor at that same time. War had come to us.

In Hong Kong, a British Colony across the border from China, we had been living outside the reach of the Sino-Japanese War for several years. However, the daily newspapers reported the ongoing war. We had been reading about the violation of Manchuria since 1932, but northeast of China was too far away for people in Hong Kong to be concerned. By 1937, with the incident at Marco Polo Bridge in Beijing, Japan had began the full scale invasion of mainland China that marked the start of the Second World War. We heard accounts and saw graphic pictures of war atrocities. Japan's drive toward and subsequent rape of Nanking was reported in gruesome detail.

I had a frightening sense of what war was about when Guangzhou too fell to the Japanese and refugees by the thousands poured across the border into the New Territories in Kowloon. My parents sent a truck full of bags of rice to aid them. I saw homeless and hungry people sleeping at the roadside, living with animals in sheds and in open fields. These people were fortunate, I was told, for they had been able to escape with their lives and some even with their families. Millions of people in China could not escape, and were dying of starvation or suffering torture and death in the war zones. In September, 1939, when Warsaw fell to the Nazis in Poland, I also heard detailed descriptions on the radio of the war-ravaged city and the suffering of its people. War everywhere had carved an indelible image in my young mind. Now, war had arrived in Hong Kong! Staring at the smoke rising on the Kowloon side of the harbor, I was frozen with anxiety. What was going to happen to us?

Steps had to be taken immediately. My parents began to pack their valuables, my father withdrew as much money as he could from the bank, and brother Yingjim joined Uncle Liu to buy whatever provisions were available. Our house, situated next to a police station at the edge of the Harbor, was considered more vulnerable for attack, so my parents decided to move our family to the basement of a friend's house on the hillside.

We stayed in that basement during the two-weeks-long siege of Hong Kong. Daily, shrill sounds of shelling screamed across the air followed by the concussion of an explosion. "Wee . . . Boom." "Wee . . . Boom." Metal pipes, stored in the basement ten deep, running the full length of the walls and stacked up almost to the ceiling, acted as shields. The individual pipes, with a diameter of about four inches, also served as safe deposits: Mother put money, jewelry, and important papers inside. The pipes dampened the sound of the shelling and bombardment, so we felt relatively secure even though the neighborhood was shelled continuously. Sitting on or between these pipes, we hid ourselves in this basement, fearful and helpless, day and night.

Our only hope was that the Hong Kong garrison could resist the attack so we would not be captured by the Japanese.

Once, during a lull in the shelling, Yingjim and I opened the front door to look. Across the street, two people lay motionless in the scattered rubble of their home. We were lucky to be spared, as Death literally passed by our front door.

On Christmas Eve, 1941, Hong Kong finally fell. Japanese warships streamed into the harbor, their army marched into Government Square and held triumphant victory ceremonies. British soldiers and civilians were herded into camps as prisoners of war and Chinese were treated as conquered people — tortured, killed and raped at will by Japanese soldiers. Our lives were no longer under our control.

The sense of danger and helplessness turned into panic and rage. My world had been turned upside down; there was no more school, no more friends, no more freedom. We did not venture outside for fear of the Japanese soldiers. My father had no work, for his taxicab business had been confiscated and all his taxicabs appropriated without any compensation. We tried to stay alive as best we could. Survival meant staying out of the way of the Japanese soldiers, because they would torture and kill without any reason. Survival meant finding enough food for the family and not getting sick or wounded because medical care was unavailable. As a child, I did not fully understand the extent of the humiliation of a conquered people, but I now experienced enough to resent it bitterly. Hatred of the conqueror was so deeply impressed on my young psyche that I have carried the burden all my life. I still cannot forgive the Japanese for their cruelties.

By the spring of 1942, my mother was making plans for the future. She would not have her children living under the Japanese; she would not let us remain out of school, uneducated.

Whatever the difficulties, she decided, we children had to be sent to free China to continue our schooling. She contacted her father in our ancestral village, Far Yuen, near Guangzhou, and asked if she could send her family. My grandfather was more than willing to accommodate her wishes. Her plan was that once we were in the village, her father would be able to smuggle us into free China.

Many people in Hong Kong had gradually moved back to their ancestral villages in China because there was no more trade or work in the city. Due to shortages of food and supplies, the Japanese encouraged the populace to disperse, to travel to occupied China. So with my father staying behind in Hong Kong to keep an eye on properties and business opportunities, my determined mother, then in her late thirties, took her substantial savings and sent all nine of her children back to her village in China, the first step in the journey to free China.

This meant not just "going home to mama." It meant crossing the no-man's-land between the war zones, braving the bandits and guerrillas operating there. Once in free China, moreover, all of her children would be directly in the front line of the war with Japan, now aggressively invading southern China. No place was safe from bombing or occupation, China was virtually defenseless. But my mother was insistent that her children continue their education, that they not live under the Japanese as conquered people without pride or dignity. Her courage, foresight and unwavering belief in education enabled us to live in free China for three and half years to continue our schooling. That changed all our lives forever, for without the continued studies in these years, we would definitely not be able to qualify for matriculation in universities later, shattering all dreams for higher education.

In separate groups of three or four, to make us less conspicuous, we began our journey by taking the overnight steamer from Hong Kong to Guangzhou. I went with younger brother Yingchou, age eleven, and elder sister Waifong, age fifteen. With my mother's brother Uncle Liu leading us, we joined other passengers for an overnight trip in a steamer headed upstream for Guangzhou. Then we took an hour-long bus ride to my grandfather's village of Far Yuen. There we settled in and waited for an opportune time to cross into free China.

Uncle Liu soon left the village. I later learned that he met with a faithful employee of my father's who knew a great deal about automobile repairs. This employee and Yingjim had carried a valuable cylinder-boring machine and other automobile parts from Hong Kong to Guangzhou. The three of them smuggled these into free China and opened a small auto repair business in the wartime Guangdong provincial capital of Shaoquan, establishing a source of income for the family there.

The border between free China and the occupied areas was a no-man's land. Whoever had the most guns at the moment was in control. Those without guns suffered. Since the Japanese did not have the resources to govern the territories taken from the Chinese government, many indeterminate skirmishes took place among the Japanese and guerrillas left in charge. These troops usually depended on robbing the people to survive; the official Chinese government had withdrawn without leaving provisions for the soldiers. Travelers were in danger not only from the soldiers but also from bandits, who, with their intimate knowledge of the region, knew exactly which travelers had the most to offer and either blackmailed them or robbed them clean. Then there were the ordinary merchants, who ran the border crossings smuggling goods from one zone to the other, making huge profits because of the scarcity and different demands in each zone. These goods included grains, gasoline, guns and ammunition, auto parts, and such daily necessities as clothing, cooking oil, and salt. The businessmen and their merchandise had to be very heavily protected, mostly by hired guns. Fortunately, as the war with Japan had been going on for several years, a kind of coexistence had built up between these groups, an "honor among thieves" system. The bottom line, as always, was money: whoever could pay the price could get what he wanted.

My maternal grandfather was a village elder at the time. He owned a brick kiln and was respected in the village for his success as well as his wisdom. His house was situated in a small family compound, with separate houses for his two married sons, all built against the hillside facing green rice fields. At the front of my grandfather's house there was a large concrete patio where children, dogs, chickens and other animals could roam and where everyone gathered after dinner to gossip and discuss village affairs. After the harvest, this large patio would be used to spread out grains to dry in the sun.

For the month that Yingchou, Waifong and I waited there, we stayed at our second uncle's spacious house on the left side of the courtyard. Daily, we were given simple chores such as shelling peas and cutting vegetables. On weekly market days, we were taken to visit the marketplace and were treated to lunch in the great dim sum restaurant usually occupied only by men. Waifong and I were tolerated because we were children. Otherwise, we just played with our two cousins who were about our age. We ran down to the rice fields, played by the pond, followed the river to the bend and explored everywhere freely as children do.

There were no Japanese soldiers stationed in the village. My memories of rural China reflect only peace and enchantment. I was totally captivated by the beauty of the wide-open green rice fields and the bamboo groves, the sound of roosters in the morning and the sight of buffalos working in the fields. These experiences matched precisely the poetic descriptions I had memorized since first grade. Even though we had no running water, no electricity, no indoor plumbing or any kind of sewage system, I did not feel the inconvenience. My grandfather and his family had to supplement their diet with yam, taro and other root vegetables because there was not enough rice. I thought it a novel idea, not a hardship. The poetic notions I harbored enabled me to enjoy the romance and tranquility of the village and must have blinded me to the harshness of life in rural China. Undoubtedly, Grandfather sheltered us from the hardship as well. After all these years, I remember only the beauty and the peacefulness of farm life in China.

I had no idea how much it cost to get us safely into free China. I only knew that one bright morning in late May, Grandpa informed us that we were going to travel, that we should pack up the clothes we had brought with us and carry the lunch he had prepared. We would travel a long way, he said. In case the journey was too difficult, he had arranged to have someone carry Yingchou and me in two baskets on the ends of a long pole resting on the carrier's shoulders.

"You will have to walk or travel this way the whole day," he told us. "Uncle Liu will meet you in Chingyuen. Just let the grown-ups take care of things. Don't be afraid." He then lead us to the market place, handed us over to some strangers, and bade us farewell.

That was the last time I saw my kind, gentle, wise maternal grandfather. He died of old age during the war, before we had a chance to meet again.

Yingchou, Waifong, and I left the village with these

strangers, a group of ten people. Sometimes walking, sometimes being carried, we were on the road the whole day, not even stopping to eat, just munching on lunch as we walked. We passed small villages, rice fields, garrisons and market places. Along the way, I saw dead bodies on the side of the road, one with the flesh of his leg cut out, exposing the thigh bone. Once soldiers stopped us and the grown-ups negotiated with them, as we waited along the roadside. I don't remember being afraid, but it was a strange and difficult journey. I had never walked for a whole day before.

We arrived at an inn in Chingyuan after dark and met Uncle Liu there. After dinner, we went to bed, too tired even to celebrate the fact that we had arrived in free China without any incident. The next day, we got up early and boarded a large junk to begin our journey up river to the free wartime provincial capital of Guangdong Province, the city of Shaoquan.

I had never been in one of these junks before. Even with its sails up, men still had to go ashore with a big rope to pull the boat upstream beside a towpath on the hillside. These men were barefooted and wore only shorts. They chanted in unison while they pulled the rope on their shoulders, and I could see sweat dripping from their brows and shiny bodies. At the same time, men on a narrow walkway on both sides of the junk were putting long poles into the river bottom and straining against their shoulders to push the junk upriver. They walked from bow to stern, then lifted the poles from the river, ran to the front of the junk, and started the process again. This they did with rhythm in the hot humid weather of Southern China for hours at a time. After all these years, this way of river travel still exists vividly in my memory and, I am told, continues yet in some parts of China. But even as a child, I thought, "there must be a better way of taking a boat upriver."

We continued up the northern tributary of the Pearl River. After several days, we arrived in the bustling wartime provincial capital of Shaoquan. Uncle Liu led us to our brother Yingjim, who was situated in an auto-repair shop on the main street of this crowded city. With the smuggled machine from Hong Kong, Yingjim and a friend had established a busy auto-repair business as planned.

As soon as Yingjim saw us, he began to sob. "What am I going to do with you? There is no room to house all of us! The city is under evacuation orders. Where are we going to go?" The four of us stood there crying, not with joy but with confusion, sadness and bewilderment. We did not have a home to go to.

Mr. Teng, Yingjim's partner, interceded.

"Hey, come on. This is a happy occasion, not a time for tears. Let's call the Colonel."

Mr. Teng's friend, a colonel in the KMT army, did have room in his house and would let us stay until we found something else. So we spent that summer of 1942 in the villa of the Colonel with his two wives and children. I saw another facet of Chinese family life that I would never forget.

It was common then — in fact almost mandatory — for a successful Chinese man to have several wives to show his wealth or prominence. In theory, these wives would all live together under the authority of the first wife, who had the respect of her husband as well as that of society at large. In reality, however, the concubine who had the husband's affection, (usually the newest one) would be much more powerful than the first wife. Just imagine the tension and infighting among these wives and their children! Fortunately, my own mother, a strong and wise woman, had kept my father from having any concubines, so we children were luckily spared such unpleasant situations in our house.

The Colonel's first wife was a pretty woman in her thirties, quiet and with a kind disposition. She had two small children — a boy of seven, and a younger girl — who, from all appearances, seemed to be happy children. The Colonel's concubine was the younger sister of this first wife. She was pretty, vivacious, energetic, and talkative. She talked to us children and played games with us while her sister was busy managing the house and the maids. Every afternoon around four o'clock, I remember, the first wife entered the kitchen to supervise dinner preparations. The concubine then stopped playing with us and went to her room.

At around five o'clock, the Colonel came home and greeted everyone happily. Then he disappeared into the concubine's room and the children were told not to disturb him. During this period the first wife changed. She started to scold or even beat the children, ordered the maids around, and grumbled at everything. The tension in the house was unbearable. When the Colonel and the concubine emerged from her room, dinner was served. I will never forget the hatred on the face of the first wife as she ate. No matter how the Colonel tried to keep things pleasant, dinner was a very unhappy event every night. The children just sat there and ate, not making any sound lest they be scolded. How different from the joy of sharing stories and poems that our family so often experienced at mealtime.

I spent that summer of 1942 taking examinations and filing applications to different schools for entrance to seventh grade. In China, the education system followed the pattern of six years of primary school, three years of junior high school, three years of senior high school and four years of university. Since I was in the first semester of sixth grade in December 1941, Yingjim decided that I should enter high school at the seventh grade in September, 1942. He also decided that Yingchou, who was younger and had finished only half a year of fifth grade, should also try to enter the seventh grade with me in first-year junior high school, because it would be difficult to find a boarding school for him as an elementary school student.

Good boarding high schools existed in the area at the time. These were prestigious schools originally founded in Guangzhou by foreign missionaries but largely administered by Chinese educators. The schools had moved with the provincial government out of the occupied area when Guangzhou fell to the Japanese, to northern Guangdong province in free China. The quality and reputation of these schools were maintained because most of the faculty and administrators also came to the new locations. Competition to enter these schools was fierce. Yingchou and I took qualifying examinations for different schools and eagerly awaited the results. On the prescribed date at the prescribed location, we checked the outcome and found both our names listed on the big poster as being accepted in the private school of our choice. Yingjim also was accepted as a transfer student to be a junior at the government-administered Chungshan University located in Pengsek, the same town, as our boarding school. Waifong was accepted as a boarding student in a government-sponsored high school in Lockchong, about an hour's train ride north of Shaoquan. Thus, by September we were able to continue our education as well as solve the difficult problem of housing.

· 8 ·

Rural China

*I*n early September 1942, the three of us — Yingjim, Yingchou and I — took the train north from Shaoquan to Pengsek, just south of the Hunan Province border. The ride took about three and a half hours, stopping at several small stations on the way. We wound slowly along the Northern River and soon went into undeveloped countryside covered with lush green pines and peppered with the changing orange and red colors of deciduous trees. There were hardly any houses; only dense forests, high mountains, and deep gorges, the most exciting and awe-inspiring rural scenery I had ever seen. Such mountainous landscape, so different from the familiar Pearl River Delta in southern China, imperceptibly intensified the discomfort that I felt on my way to a new life.

No cars or buses were waiting at the small train station, not even rickshaws or tricycles. Yingjim hired a laborer to carry our luggage, and we walked for an hour to the school.

After registering at the business office near the entrance, Yingjim went with Yingchou to the boys' dormitory down the road. The middle-aged housekeeper told me to come with her. Carrying my belongings, I followed her past a long row of classroom buildings on our left. On the other side, facing these buildings, stretched a vast open field with a flagpole near the road. The housekeeper lead me down a steep dirt track at the end of the classrooms, through a green valley of rice paddies, and up the next hillside. There stood the newly constructed women's dormitories. I was assigned a lower bunk near the front door in the long, rectangular, one-story building for junior high girls. The dormitories for senior girls were located further up the hill. Below us were several smaller buildings scattered along the mud path. She told me I could start unpacking my belongings on my bunk. That small act began my boarding school experience.

Two rows of bunk beds lined both walls in the building I was in. A central hallway about eight feet wide ran the length of the building and separated the rows. Some girls had already unpacked. There was just enough space between the bunks to walk past each other. Through the tall windows between the parallel bunks one could see the trees and yellow earth outside. We had no tables, chairs, nor dressers but stored our suitcases under the bottom bunk, sliding them out as we needed to fetch clothing or other items, like pulling out a drawer.

The buildings were built simply with stucco plastered on woven bamboo frames one story tall. There was no electricity, running water, central heating nor air conditioning. Outside, a flight of steep, narrow stairs going downhill led to the dining hall. A hundred yards below that stood the toilet and bathhouse complex. Toilets had no seats nor flushing mechanisms but consisted of a big hole with a huge collecting container underneath. In the bathhouse next door, where each evening the housekeeper ladled out hot water into our individual buckets for bathing, I found no showers nor washbasins nor running water, just two long low shelves along the wall to put our buckets. Soap was a prized commodity, and for shampoo we pounded cakes of a dried herb and soaked the crumbs in hot water to make lather for washing our hair. Washing my long hair was a particularly difficult task because up to now my hair had always been shampooed for me by others.

In warm weather, we walked twenty minutes downhill beyond the dormitory to the river to bathe and do our laundry in the fast-running river. That was most enjoyable. We always carried a pail of water back for the morning wash so we would not have to stand in line for the housekeeper to parcel out water.

None of the walkways or steps up the hillside was paved. In good weather, the soil was dusty; when it rained, the yellow wet mud was everywhere, sticking to our shoes with each step. Every so often we had to stop and scrape the accumulated inch of mud off the soles of our shoes so we could walk on again. The slippery steps caused many painful falls as daily we trotted down the hill from dormitory, across the narrow path between rice paddies, and up the other hill to classroom and back.

This rural China where I found myself was totally different from the city where I grew up. Here my eyes feasted on trees, green fields, rice paddies, and small narrow paths, not apartment buildings or blacktop traffic lanes. This was a world apart from my familiar world of crowded tenement houses, electric lights and noisy automobiles. There were hardly any automobiles anywhere.

And it was quiet. One noticed the silence right away. Sounds came from singing birds, rustling leaves, barking dogs, and crowing roosters, a contrast to the jarring sounds of automobile horns or people clamoring. If one listened carefully, one could hear the earth humming, insects buzzing in the spring and summer.

I had never seen a rice plant before, never learned where rice came from, even though we ate it daily. (History repeated itself years later when my young son knew only that milk came in a carton from the grocery store down the street.) Living among the rice paddies was a new and fascinating experience. In the spring, farmers by the hundreds went down to the paddies, bending low as they placed young plants neatly in the field, row after row of bright green appearing overnight. In the summer, the flooded paddies started to sing at night with the incessant croaking of frogs. As the plants grew taller, they swayed gently with the wind, small waves of a verdant sea. By autumn, the heavy heads of golden grains on long yellow stalks dipped wearily toward the earth. After harvest, when the fields were drained and the plants cut, the dark earth revealed itself once again. To release the grains, the farmers hit the stalks on a simple bamboo surface following an ancient rhythm that mesmerized me. For a city girl, this seasonal change was pure magic.

Many other aspects of country life were new to me. We used candles, oil lamps and kerosene lanterns at night in study halls. We drew water from the well or carried it in small pails from the river. I had to learn how to throw the bucket down the well so it would fall open-end first to take in water instead of floating on top of it. Again and again, I tried to throw the bucket so it would dip under the surface and fill with water. At the same time, I had to hold onto the rope lest it follow the bucket down into the well.

In the outhouse toilet, where the "night-soil" was saved for farmers as fertilizer, the smell was unbearable and one dared not look down the small opening at the worms gyrating in the human waste. In the winter, when the temperature often dipped below freezing, our layers of clothing were topped, day and night, by a padded jacket filled with cotton or silk. During the summer, only our profuse sweat kept us cool.

The village people were not educated nor "street-smart."

Their rhythm of life was simple. They rose early, before sunrise, and went to bed right after sundown. Farmers, men and women alike, worked in the fields while the daylight lasted. They ate two meals a day, one before noon and one before dusk. By age-old tradition, extended families lived together; grandmothers and older relatives took care of the young. Children began taking on responsibilities early, caring for younger siblings and doing such simple chores as delivering meals to the field. Formal education was considered a luxury.

Our life at school was highly regulated in military precision. Bugle calls woke us up at 6 a.m. We washed, dressed, and made our beds military fashion: all four corners of our cotton-stuffed blanket had to be folded in ninety-degree angles. Two hard-covered books were used to smooth the top edges into sharp folds. At 7 a.m., the captain of the dormitory blew a whistle to announce the arrival of the faculty inspector. By the time the inspector stepped in the front door, we were all standing at attention at the foot of our beds. Demerits were given to anyone who was not ready or who did not measure up to the inspector's standard of neatness.

Only then, after the inspections, could we go to breakfast. In the dining hall, large buckets of hot rice porridge were waiting in the center isle for us to ladle into our individual bowls. After we ate, we dashed madly across the hill to the parade grounds for the flag-raising ceremony.

The whole school of about three hundred students gathered in the parade grounds in military formation, boys and girls in separate divisions, with the junior high students dressed in scout uniforms and the senior high students in military uniforms. After the platoon leader called the roll, she marched up to the captain, saluted smartly and reported our presence. When all was considered in good order, we stood at attention and sang our current national anthem, the KMT party anthem.

In unison, we sang at the top of our voices: "The three People's Principles, our party adheres, to build the republic, to achieve one world . . ." Then the bugle sounded. Following the captain's shouted orders, we raised our right hands to salute as the national flag of "blue skies, white sun, and red earth," symbol of our beloved country, slowly crawled up the flag pole. I still remember the pride I felt as I watched that flag fluttering in the wind, proud that I was no longer a colonial subject of the British monarch, living in the colony of Hong Kong, but a free citizen in the Republic of China. Afterwards, a faculty member, usually the head of the "Discipline Department," made an announcement or two and then we were marched, platoon by platoon, to the auditorium for the morning assembly.

On Mondays, the morning assembly was a patriotic rally. We started by standing and reciting the last will and testament of the founder of the Republic, Dr. Sun Yet-Sen. The document was written in classical Chinese that was easy for me to understand, thanks to my classical education. This weekly recitation detailed his experience in forty years of revolution against the Qing Dynasty, seeking equal treatment for China from foreign countries and freedom for her people. "I deeply believe that in order to achieve our goals, we must awaken our people and cooperate with nations that befriend us with equality to engage in this effort. Our revolution has not yet succeeded. Comrades! We must continue to strive." Before long, I had this memorized. I was no longer an obedient Confucian scholar but a free republican, following Dr. Sun Yet-Sen, fighting for the revolution.

Always, there were speeches. We were told that because we were educated, we were the inheritors of China, the hope of our people; we must save our country at this dangerous cross-road. China and her people's destiny rested on our shoulders! We also praised Chiang Kai-Shek and other leaders for fighting the Japanese, for "winning" the war. We reaffirmed our faith in our country and in the final victory over the Japanese invaders, firmly convinced that justice was on our side. The Monday program was serious and heroic. Besides feeling lucky to be alive and educated, I also deeply felt the debt I owed China in her dangerous hours. Instead of aspiring to serve the Emperor, I would now serve the Republic of China.

On other mornings, the assembly was a religious service, conducted by the resident Protestant minister. We started with a hymn, followed by prayers and some profession of faith to Jesus Christ or Almighty God. The minister or some teacher gave a sermon or read a lesson from the Bible, and we ended with more singing of hymns. On Easter and Christmas, we had more elaborate celebrations.

These short, pleasant services were my first exposure to Christianity. Since my parents followed the Chinese religion of ancestor worship, I had never attended church and was unfamiliar with Christian rituals or doctrines. My father considered the Christian preachers to be charlatans or swindlers and did not associate with them. He had also warned us against religious fanaticism, urging us to follow the Confucian doctrine of "the Way of the Mean," that everything should be done in moderation and not in fervent extremes. If he had known that our education included this Baptist religious indoctrination, he probably would have objected to our attending that school.

In my youthful curiosity, however, I found the Christian rituals fascinating. I loved the hymns, a new kind of music for me. Before then, I had been exposed only to Cantonese opera, with its well-written classical verses and drama, and I had learned to sing many of the arias. Chinese music has an entirely different scale and is not harmonized. Christian hymns written in Western music introduced me to harmonies, and the compassionate verses roused my emotions. Every time I heard "Jesus loves me, this I know," I felt reassured, and "Onward, Christian soldiers" never failed to stir my fighting spirit. Every morning in assembly, I eagerly learned these hymns and sang them with all my heart.

The idea of praying to a loving and all-encompassing God was more difficult for me to comprehend, because all the gods I knew were stern and judgmental and fearsome. Though I found it soothing to close my eyes and talk to a God who would grant my wishes if I tried hard enough, I had difficulty trying to accept that there was only one such magnificent God. Didn't we need more than one god to care for all of our needs? The Chinese always had more gods than anyone could count. There was a separate god in everything on earth, as well as in heaven, to take care of things. Why should Christians be allowed only one God? How could He be omnipresent? How could He take care of so many people?

The horrifying doctrine of a hell was not new to me: the Chinese folk religion also had vivid descriptions of that. Any temple worthy of its name would have panoramas depicting scenes of hell inhabited by suffering, wicked people. One would go to hell if one did hideous deeds in life. I had seen these depictions and had taken the warning seriously. In any case, my young mind, inculcated with Confucian doctrines, was not concerned about life after death or the eternal salvation of my soul; for Confucius had said: "I do not yet know about life, how can I know about death?" Most Confucian scholars never troubled themselves much with life after death.

The Christian belief I found most difficult to accept was the assumption that all of us are born sinners and have to beg interminably for forgiveness and redemption. I never understood why one was born "a sinner" and that the "original sin" should remain with us through life. Confucians believe all humans are born innocent and good, and that environment is what influences them to be bad. I never felt the need for redemption, only the need not to become bad and lose my human goodness. The idea still fascinates me that people willingly brand themselves sinners and spend their lives seeking redemption.

I think this basic Confucian belief that men are born good, not sinners, an idea that prevailed in China for two thousand some years, must have presented a real stumbling block to the missionaries attempting to convert the Chinese.

I was not the only student learning Christian doctrines for the first time. Not many of us became believers, although some did accept Christ before the end of the year. I remember clearly the baptism rituals by the river on Easter Sunday in 1943. Some ten students in simple white gowns stood by the river bank with the minister, facing a large gathering of students and faculty. We were directed to sing certain hymns, and prayers were said for all of us, especially for the people gathered around the minister. Then the minister waded into the river. One by one, the students in white gowns were led to him. He raised his right hand and blessed each before he immersed the student's body in the river. Then we sang more hymns — the refrains of "Alleluia" still ring in my ears. Afterwards, the minister told us that these new Christians were saved and would go to heaven when they died. Even to a nonbeliever, that was a moving experience. It must be very comforting to know that someone loves you and will send you to a beautiful Heaven when your days on earth are done.

After the morning assembly, whatever its content, we went

to our classes. Each class lasted fifty minutes followed by ten minutes of recess. A different teacher came to the classroom each hour. We always stood when the teacher came into the room and would not sit down until he told us to do so. At the end of the fourth period, the girls went back to the other hill for their lunch, which consisted of rice and vegetables with an occasional piece of meat. We did not say grace before meals, but sat stiffly at our places in military style until someone in charge barked "Kei Dung," meaning "Begin." Our daily routines were formed by military discipline.

After the hour lunch break, we were back in the classroom for three more periods of classes. That year, for my assigned courses, I had Chinese, English, history and — for the first time in my life — biology, mathematics, civics, geography, music, military science and physical education. Most of the subjects met for three periods a week, except for civics, music, military science and physical education, which were taught once a week. The last two were taught on the parade grounds or the playing fields. In Pengsek, for the first time, I had lessons in military formation and marching, also in playing baseball and basketball. Subjects like these were never in the curriculum in my classical elementary school in Hong Kong. In that school for girls, we were taught to do embroidery and knitting, not marching and athletics!

After classes, we had a couple of hours before dinner to relax and to pursue extracurricular activities such as play rehearsals, chorale practices, and baseball games. After dinner, we were all required to be back in the classroom between 7 and 9 PM to do homework. A teacher stayed with us to check attendance and to help with homework. For this study period, the school provided acetylene lamps in the classrooms, two to a room, hanging high from the ceiling. Frequently, the acetylene lamps would be blown out, and then we had to wait for the maintenance man to come to change the silk "bulb" before we could continue our studies. For getting around between buildings in the dark, we carried our own small, glass-enclosed oil lamps, which were lighted by lifting one of the sliding glass sides to light the wick inside.

On Saturdays, we had only the four morning periods of classes. The afternoon was spent on "free activities." Several of us worked on the school paper, which was written, edited, and copied by hand, then pinned up on the bulletin board on Mondays. Sometimes we took a walk in the surrounding areas within the campus limits. That's how I discovered the most beautiful cherry tree grove a short distance away from our living quarters. On one Sunday a month, after church services, we were "let out" to go to the village marketplace, an hour's walk away, or to the small business area at the railroad station, in the opposite direction. This privilege was granted only to students of good behavior with no demerits during the month. If the student wasn't back by five o'clock in the afternoon for check-in at the registrar's office, the privilege would be taken away for the next month. We were all careful about keeping each other on time, for we did so love this rare outing, when we could stuff ourselves with dim sum and other wonderful food or shop for delicacies to supplement our meager meals in school. Along with modern Chinese, nationalism, and Christianity, in this, my first year in China, I also learned the importance of food.

Generally, I found life in school difficult and harsh. Hygienic conditions were less than perfect and medical care was minimal. From mosquito or some other insect bites, I unfortunately developed a boil on my lower right leg shortly after I arrived at the boarding school. In that pre-antibiotics time, the infection simply would not go away. Every two or three days, I went to the school nurse, who removed the dressing, cleansed the open wound with hydrogen peroxide, and applied new gauze. For most of that year, I limped along the best I could, often in pain. The wound finally healed, but to this day I carry an inch-wide scar on my right leg.

As this was the first time I attended a co-educational school, I had difficulties in getting used to the teasing by boys. They targeted clothing, demeanor and appearance for their criticism and comments, which I found trivial. To my surprise, I also found some of the teasing very mean-spirited.

Even though I made many friends and kept busy involving myself with school activities — for which I received the Service Award for Junior Girls that January — I longed for home, my large family and a more familiar way of life. Christmas vacation that year was most unbearable. Everyone else in the student body went home. But Yingjim, who was attending Chungshan University in town as a sophomore, came for a visit and told us that Yingchou and I could not leave for Christmas vacation because he had no place to house us. Our mother, still in Hong Kong, had just given birth to her last child, and we had no home to go to. As a favor, the school let us stay on the premises for the two weeks. So Yingchou and I stayed in the unheated, empty dormitories while our fellow students went home to their families.

Heartbroken though we were, the situation could have been worse. In early January, the Japanese made an extensive bombing raid on Shaoquan where we would have gone for the Christmas break. The defenseless city burned for days, and many people lost their lives. We might well have been among them.

· 9 ·

Retreat

*M*y mother finally arrived in Shaoquan with her youngest baby, Yingbun, early in 1943. Soon, she realized that Yingchou was having health problems and was not doing well in Pengsek.

She immediately ordered his transfer when the second semester began in February, to another missionary school, Wah Ying Middle School, located in Shaoguan. He did not board there but became a day student living at home with Mother. No matter how crowded the house was, Mother wanted him home so she could keep an eye on him. I remained in Pengsek until June and finished the school year there.

That summer in 1943, fourteen months after leaving Hong Kong, I happily went "home" to Shaoguan to my mother's rented two-bedroom house. All nine of us were there with her. Even though I had to sleep across the bed with four of my siblings at night, I did not mind. During the day, I learned to care for my infant brother Yingbun, whom I met for the first time, while my mother started to have a house built for the family nearby.

We faced a number of devastating events during that time. I remember a flood early in the summer when we had to move everything from the house to higher grounds on the hill behind the house. I also remember frequent air-raid warnings, when we had to run with all our energy, carrying the younger children, into the air raid shelters dug into the hillside a mile or so away. There we crowded in the stuffy cave and waited anxiously, until the all-clear signal sounded, not knowing whether we would still have a home after the air raid.

Just as our new house was nearing completion, our next-door neighbor, a prominent man with high ranking in the military, decided that our house was better and bigger than the one he was building, and demanded that we change houses with him. My mother could do nothing but comply. That was wartime China.

Later that summer, Yingjim suddenly fell ill with typhoid fever. With great difficulty, we transported him to the River West Hospital. Twice a day, evening and morning, mother and I walked an hour and half to the hospital to visit him. During his worst days, I stayed in the hospital to keep cold compresses on his fevered forehead, helping to lower his body temperature. For days, I sat listening to his delirium, often frantically running into the hall to call for help. The western-trained Dr. Lu Shuisun eventually saved his life. Yingjim recovered after a long stay in the hospital.

On our long walks to the hospital, mother told me the story of how, luckily, she had put aside enough money so we could afford to put Yingjim in the best hospital and provide him with the best medical care. Otherwise, she said, he would be dead. I had no real understanding of the heavy burden my mother was carrying at the time, but the lesson of saving money for rainy days stayed with me throughout my life.

In the late Fall of 1943, the family moved into the new house. I did not go back to Pengsek but transferred to Wah Ying Middle School in Shaoguan as a boarding student with Waifong while Yingchou remained a day student, living at home and walking the hour and half to school every day. For me, life in the eighth grade was pretty much the same as the year before, with two exceptions. One was the campus; no longer in the rural area of China, we had electricity, plumbing, and some modern conveniences. The campus was also much smaller, with brick dormitories and classrooms built around a paved courtyard, no more muddy paths or steep hillsides to climb. The biggest difference though was that my mother was living nearby — I could go home on weekends to see her and to enjoy home cooking and other comforts.

The major drawback was that the school was situated in the provincial capital, not in the wilderness in Pengsek, and therefore was a target for Japanese bombs. Air raids were frequent and sometimes devastating. Sirens wailed as we studied in our classrooms. Each time, we had to interrupt our lessons and run to the air-raid shelter some distance beyond the school, staying until the all-clear signal sounded. Even though only once or twice did we actually hear bombs exploding nearby, it was a frightening experience. When the bombings stopped, we courageously went back to our classrooms and resumed our lessons.

Chemistry was our science subject that year, and we had a serious, knowledgeable teacher who taught us the magic of chemical reactions. My lifelong love of chemistry began there in war-torn China between bombing raids by the Japanese. I was fascinated at being able to put into equations the reactions of molecules, indeed of stuff of life itself. My enchantment with the subject began with atoms, things that one could not see but that could explain mysterious natural phenomena so precisely. The periodic table completely captured my imagination. I also found it great fun to be able to balance chemical equations to predict experiments. The fact that a small piece of metal, sodium, dropped into a container of ordinary water, could be depended on to explode with great force was more bewitching to me than any display of fireworks. And one could even write a balanced equation to explain it!

We also began studying algebra, a subject I cherished because it put me out of the misery of solving difficult arithmetic problems. It was so much easier! However, I had a difficult time with both trigonometry and geometry. My mind seemed unable to form spacial relationships between lines, and forms remained flat surfaces in my imagination.

By the end of my eighth grade, in the summer of 1944, the Japanese began their big drive to invade southern China. The population in Shaoguan began again to evacuate. My mother decided to send two daughters and three younger sons back to occupied Guangzhou where life was more stable and they could go to school under the puppet Chinese government established under Wong Jin-Wai. The ones who would leave were Waifong (19), Yingchou (11), Waitong (10), Yingsheung (9) and Yingkwong (6).

I remember helping my mother pack paper currency into five gallon containers of square tin cans with a hinged top. These were converted from the sturdy metal cans used for delivering gasoline or diesel fuel for cars or trucks. Because of the runaway inflation during the war, a large amount of paper money was needed to buy anything. These cans served as convenient containers to store and secure the large quantity of needed currency. When we finished, there were three or four of these cans. My mother distributed them among the three groups in the family for evacuation.

Uncle Liu, who at the time was making a lucrative living by running the blockade between the occupied and free zones, took the five children with some other relatives south along the North River, the northern tributary of the Pearl River. They arrived safely in Guangzhou shortly. There, with the help of my maternal grandmother's slave servant who was sold to her recently, Waifong set up housekeeping and found a school for every child. She, herself, did not continue school but dutifully stayed home to care for her younger siblings. The young slave girl ran away in Guangzhou shortly after her arrival.

My mother, with her youngest son Yingbun, less than two years old at the time, left Shaoguan shortly afterward to follow them to Guangzhou, but they were stopped by the advancing Japanese army at Lingonghou, where the West River joins the Pearl River. She had to divert up the West River, the west tributary of the Pearl River, to Guilin. The family did not hear from her until months later when she showed up exhausted at the front door in Guangzhou. Yingbun had boils all over his head. When my father asked him why he did not say hello, the boy replied, "I don't know how to address you." He had not seen his father since he was a few months old and could not identify who Father was. Mother never talked about her journey on the West River. I could only guess at her hardship.

The third group, Yingjim, Waijin and I, bravely stayed in Shaoguan. Yingjim had graduated from Chungshan University by then and was employed by the provincial government. He had to stay in the city under orders. By September, Wah Ying Middle School had also evacuated with most of the faculty and students to Guilin. In order to continue my education, I had to find another school to attend for the new school year in Fall of 1944.

Skipping ninth grade, I was admitted by examination to the first semester of tenth grade, as a day student in a military senior high school across town called Chung Jen Academy. Every morning I got up before dawn, put on my military uniform and, with the help of a little oil lamp, walked several miles, crossing two floating pontoon bridges, so I would be on time to school for the morning-flag raising ceremony at seven o'clock. The trip took more than two hours one way. I must confess that I did not learn much academically at the military school but I did learn how to distinguish mud holes, water pools, and rocks on the unpaved, potholed road in the dark: mud holes were black, rocks were white, and water pools were bright. I trod very carefully among them.

Fortunately, or unfortunately depending on one's point of view, this ordeal did not last long. The Japanese did invade Shaoguan later that Fall. Yingjim, Waijin and I evacuated, along with the provincial government officials and other refugees, riding on the back of a crowded truck, just in time to escape the advancing Japanese army. As we drove out on the highway, along the East River, the east tributary of the Pearl River, we looked back and watched the fallen city burn in its full glory. The government had successfully carried out their "scorched earth" policy and burned the city before they left. We felt fortunate to have escaped with our lives.

Yingjim's orders were to evacuate along the East River to Longchuan county. Since we were traveling by car and not by boat, the highway took us northeastward into Kiangxi Province before coming back south to Quangdong Province and County Longchuan. After traveling all night, we arrived at a small town in Kiangxi Province where, I was told, the Chinese Communists had a commune.

Ever since the formation of the Chinese Communist Party in Shanghai in the 1920s, the word Communist had struck terror in the hearts of many Chinese. The Central government had made the Communist party illegal and regularly conducted campaigns to round up its members and put them to death. The final routing of the Communist army had resulted in the well-known and devastating Long March, when Mao Zedong led his remaining army west and northwest to Yenan through difficult terrains and unimaginable hardship. Most of the soldiers on that Long March perished.

But at the beginning of the war with Japan in the 1930s, the government vowed publicly to cooperate with the Communists so that, with them together, China could defeat Japan. The two parties tolerated each other in the name of national unity.

Like most young students, I had heard of the Communists and their idealistic doctrines. I first thought that the Communist principle, believing in people working together, forgetting their selfishness and greed for the common good to build a better society for all, was a wonderful idea. But after hearing some of the horror stories and propaganda from the national government about them (my father told us at one time that the Communists advocated killing everyone over thirty), I was ready to view the Communists as "bandits," as they were then called.

Both Yingjim and I were quite surprised to find that the town was not only controlled by the Communists but that Communist communes had operated there for a number of years. As we walked around, we found friendly militia patrolling the streets and directing traffic. The main thoroughfare was very clean and people were polite and orderly without the rushing and bustling that we were so accustomed to. It was a rare sight to see a town in such good order in wartime China. My impression of the Communists literally changed overnight.

In a short time, we arrived safely with the retreating government forces in Longchuan. There, for the second semester of tenth grade, in February 1945, I was enrolled in a private, non-missionary school named Chung-Tek Middle School as a boarding student. The school was located in an old temple with no campus to speak of. Faculty and students combined made up no more than forty people. It was a "fly-by night," money making concern to take advantage of the wartime chaos. I don't remember any lessons learned there. The only memory I have of that semester is yet another evacuation.

Yingjim was ordered to leave town with the provincial government to move further into the mountains of northeast Quangdong Province to Ta-jeh, in Mei County. This had been the strategy of the government, they kept moving further and further back, calling it "changing to advantageous grounds." The army would not fight the Japanese but kept retreating, would not confront the invaders. I have often thought that if China had not been so vast in territory, and if the United States had not been drawn into the War by the bombing of Pearl Harbor, China with this government policy would have been defeated and enslaved by the Japanese long ago.

This plan for evacuation was for Yingjim and Waijin to leave for Ta-jeh and for me to stay in Longchuan to finish the semester at Chung-Tek Middle School by myself. Before he and Waijin left, Yingjim gave me some money and, as a measure against the rampant inflation, several pieces of solid gold jewelry. He told me that if anything happened, I should go to Ta-jeh and look for him at the provincial government office. That was all the information I had, not even an address, for they didn't know where they would be living. Sewing the gold pieces into my clothing and holding on to the money, I stayed by myself in Longchuan, hoping that the Japanese would not come until I finished the semester. None of us questioned the wisdom of leaving me behind in the boarding school when most people were evacuated. The fact that I should continue my education seemed most important. No one seemed to realize the difficulties I had to face by myself without any family should the Japanese army advanced to Longchuan. They thought, at fifteen, I could handle it. I was thus abandoned in the name of education!

Unfortunately, that semester was never finished. In April 1945, the school told us that we had to run before the Japanese overtook the town. I had no idea what to do to get out of town, how to find transportation to Ta-jeh. There was no family, no one to help. Fortunately, in the chaos and desperation of evacuation, a schoolmate found transportation for both of us to leave town on a truck. The price was one of my gold pieces, a ring. Watching the town burning and listening to gunfire, we rode out of town just in time to escape the advancing Japanese army.

Overnight, I arrived at Ta-jeh. The town was filled with refugees and soldiers. Walking aimlessly in the central square trying to locate my brother Yingjim, I spotted my good friend Yu Shaman, a Pengsek classmate and daughter of the Commander of the Seventh War District army. It was the most welcome surprise and a big blessing to run into her at the town center. With her powerful family's assistance, she helped me get in touch with Yingjim and Waijin.

There, hiding in the high mountains of Ta-jeh, safe from Japanese attacks, we, along with the provincial government in exile, waited for the war to end. I did not attend school there, for there were not any to be found. In early August, through short-wave radios, we learned, not with regret but with great joy, about the dropping of the atomic bomb in Hiroshima and again at Nagasaki. When the news came that Japan had finally surrendered unconditionally, Yingjim and I fired a gun for celebration. That was the only time I ever handled a firearm in spite of my years of military training.

We had finally come to the end of our odyssey. The War had

ended. We no longer had to run from the Japanese, no more bombing, no more evacuations. The enemy had surrendered unconditionally! Now, we could go home to Hong Kong. Life would be normal again.

Quickly the three of us — Yingjim, Waijin and I — made arrangements to join the rest of the family. There in Guangzhou in a second floor flat, all eleven of us, my parents and their nine children, rejoiced and marveled at our luck. We had endured three and half years of a savage war. We had been scattered in separate directions, up the West River, down the North River and through the East River, to escape the advancing Japanese army and now found ourselves all alive without serious ill effects. My parents were still in their forties and young: the family could go back to Hong Kong to start all over again. It was the happiest day of our lives. We were all alive and well and living together as a family again. The family had braved the dangers of war to achieve the goal of continuing our education successfully. As soon as we found our way back to Hong Kong, we would all be able to start school again, to continue our lives. In that British colony, life would be normal, predictable, and under our control as before. True, we did not know exactly how we would start, but we knew we were much luckier than many others. We could count our blessings indeed.

More fortunate still, in going back to live in our birthplace, Hong Kong, we were spared the Communist rule that soon befell China. Still many more Chinese people would perish in that epic political struggle, and none of us could be sure that we would escape the many government persecutions had we stayed in China.

· 10 ·

Independence

Early in the morning, the roller-skating rink was empty except for a small lone figure whirling around in the large rectangular space. The little boy, no more than four years old, skated backwards, forwards and in figure eights on the smooth concrete surface, obviously enjoying himself. A man outside the rink shouted to him:

"Bunny, watch out. Don't go too fast! Be careful!"

"Yes, Papa, I will be careful. Can you change the music to a waltz, please?"

The man went into the office and changed the music. When he came out, he noticed a family waiting at the entrance and he walked quickly to let them in.

The man was my father and the little boy my youngest brother Yingbun at our skating rink in the summer of 1945 in Hong Kong.

*I*t could be considered a miracle that all eleven of us, my parents and nine children, survived unscathed the three and a half years of war in China. Even more remarkable, all the children continued their schooling. That miracle, of course, was due to my mother, who tenaciously braved all hardship to get us into free China so we could continue our education. Now that the war was over and we were back in Hong Kong, my family began to plan again.

My father owned a large garage, used to park taxicabs

before the War, in the area between Wanchai and the Central District of Hong Kong. The building had an extensive open space at ground level and offices on the second floor at one end of the property. My father made the office space into living quarters for his family, and converted the rest of the garage into an open-air roller-skating rink, open daily from ten o'clock in the morning to ten o'clock at night. Business was good, especially on weekends. Yingbun's tiny figure moving skillfully around and around became a fixture at the rink. Every night after the rink closed, I watched my father crouching on the floor, diligently patching up any broken places in the cement surface, preparing for the next day's business. My mother and the rest of the family pitched in to help whenever we could. He had no experience in the skating business, but somehow, with hard work and determination, my father made a success of it.

Gradually, with the help of Yingjim's fluent English, my father negotiated with government officials to receive back payments from the Hong Kong Government for services rendered by his taxi companies before the War. The government also restored his company's taxi licenses, so he was able to get back into that business. Still later, the Hong Kong government awarded indemnities for automobiles confiscated by the Japanese during the War, so enough funds accumulated for him to buy more taxicabs.

As usual, education was of the utmost concern for the family. One by one, from Yingchou on down, the younger children were enrolled in schools that fall. Waitong, Yingsheung and Yingkwong went to finish elementary school in the private classical school. Yingchou went to the government school to study English — no more Chinese "private" school or classical Chinese education for him.

But problems arose for the older children. Yingjim, my

eldest brother, now a university graduate, had to turn down an opportunity for graduate studies in England so he could help with my father's business. Waijin and Waifong, my two elder sisters, were considered "over-aged," too old to attend high school but not qualified for the university. They stayed home, waiting to be married or perhaps to be trained for some practical work.

I was the one with the biggest problem. My command of the English language was below the level of eleventh grade, which should be my grade. If I attended the government school as my family planned, with classes taught in English, I would have to start at seventh grade. This level was much lower than my age or self-respect deemed appropriate, as I had already finished tenth grade in China during the war. I was not willing to do it. My mother, in the meantime, felt that at least one of her daughters ought to have a high school diploma after the horrendous efforts she expended for our education. To achieve this goal, I would have to go back to China and enroll at my former high school, Wah Ying Middle School. Since I had transcripts from various schools through the tenth grade, I could enter the eleventh grade at Wah Ying, and be eligible for a high school diploma in two years. That suited me much better than having to spend five or more years in the government school before graduating.

So that September in 1945, after being home in Hong Kong for only a short time, obediently I went back to my boarding school Wah Ying Middle School in China, happy to enroll in the eleventh grade. Since I had skipped a grade, I was a full year ahead of my former classmates, but we all adjusted to the fact quite easily.

The campus of Wah Ying Middle School was now reestablished in its prewar location of Fushan, on the prosperous Pearl

River Delta. Even though Fushan was near Guangzhou and had been open to foreigners for trade since the 1840's, life in that tiny county remained much the same as it had been more than a hundred years ago. Not much had changed. People still made their living the same way.

Life in the school was much like in the Wah Ying in Shaoquan. I was now very much accustomed to living in a boarding school and found it pleasant and exciting. I had no trouble fitting in. The routine we followed daily was also much like that in Shaoquan: morning exercise, flag raising ceremony, assembly, then classes: four in the morning and three in the afternoon. I took courses in Chinese, English, analytical geometry, history, civics, geography, chemistry, music and physical education, but no more military training. As usual, I did not find the school work difficult and had much time to involve myself in extracurricular activities, in the drama club, the school paper, etc. I also served as a class officer.

As a community service, the school initiated a teaching program for the townspeople in the town of Fushan. Two evenings a week, several of us students walked through the narrow alleys to a nearby temple, where children of all ages were gathered, sitting on long wooden benches, waiting for us to teach them how to read. This semi-rural area of southern China offered no compulsory education nor any educational facilities. Our school's voluntary effort was the only opportunity these children had for learning to read.

I did the best I could to show the peasant children how to recognize the Chinese characters, and taught them how each character was first formed three thousand years ago from a picture drawing and then later transformed into the present writing. As I explained what each of the ideograms means, and how these words could convey ideas, their faces lit up. The children were most eager, and I could see that literacy worked magic with them. The experience introduced me to the satisfaction of helping others, taught me the delight of teaching and the pleasure of being able to share my knowledge. I will never forget the gratitude the students and their families expressed at the end of that year.

It was also during this period of my life that my thinking turned radical. It came about through the guidance of our teacher in Chinese literature, Mr. Lai, a mild-mannered young man of about twenty-eight with horn-rim glasses. His serious facial expression gave the impression that he was constantly besieged by problems. He taught classical Chinese and modern literature, my favorite subjects. We often discussed turbulent current events and the dire social and economic conditions in postwar China. A few of us gravitated to his liberal thinking.

This kind and gentle teacher introduced me to books on Marx and Lenin, along with publications on the current heated debate on Chinese politics. The ideologies of Communism and Socialism were virtually unknown to me until then, but I immersed myself in writings of social organization, political and economic theories. I read about "dialectic materialism, unifying contradictions," and the ideals of Socialism. I followed the fervent debate between Capitalism and Communism raging at the time among intellectuals who were looking desperately for a way to save China. In the period after the War, day by day, inflation soared. Chinese social and economic conditions deteriorated, government ineptness and corruption increased tenfold, and the people's discontent escalated. People were expecting a much better life after the war; instead, conditions turned worse, with the civil war starting again. The hopelessness of the situation drove thinking and concerned citizens to search for better government to help China. A new way of governing had to be found for the people. Communism, with its egalitarian theories and a goal of "from each according to his ability, to each according to his need," sounded like an ideal choice. My impressionable young mind was elated to find such a perfect system to solve China's problems. More and more, I wanted to see the realization of this utopian state.

Mr. Lai kept me supplied with all the literature he could find. He showed me periodicals and news items, and we discussed the significance of the articles. He urged me to get "involved," to subscribe to different magazines and to write articles for them. I still have a receipt he wrote for my subscription to twelve issues of *Public Opinion Weekly*, dated March 27, 1946, for 480 yuan. These and other publications by the left-wing press, to the extent that they were allowed to circulate by the government at the time, fueled my idealism and infused my life with an exciting new purpose. I vowed that when I finished high school, I should go north to Beijing for university studies, join the Communist party, and participate in the Revolution to save China. Suddenly, my life took on new meaning, new direction in pursuit of this noble goal.

There were fellow students who held the same ambitions and ideals as I did. We often gathered to dream and fantasize our futures, as adolescents do. In my senior year, one of my fellow students started writing poems to me in a most beautiful and imaginative way. I adored his talent in poetry and his insight into my character. His metaphors about my "flaming red pomegranate-flower-like emotion and clear crystalline, snowy white of thought" sounded rapturous and exhilarating. We spent many hours together talking about national events and literature, sharing dreams. The platonic friendship lasted a long time, even after I left Hong Kong. He stayed in China, attended the university and eventually went through the Cultural

Revolution. When I saw him recently in Guangzhou at our high school reunion, he refused, perhaps out of fear of reprisal, to talk about the events of his life since we were students so long ago. I have some idea of what he went through during the Communist rule, and consider myself fortunate not to have joined the Communist Party or to have taken part in the Revolution. Looking back, I have once again to thank my mother's uncanny intuition which mercifully spared me the price I would have had to pay had I followed my youthful dreams.

Southern China was relatively peaceful during the two years between fall 1945 and summer 1947 when I was in Fushan, even though the rest of the country, especially in the North and the Northwest, were engulfed in civil war. Famines and floods also took their toll: millions perished. I was well protected, even isolated, from the horrible effects of inflation by remaining in school, where I had the much-needed time and tranquility to recover from my war experiences. For my classmates who lived in China after 1948, however, life was very different. For some, unfortunately, it was fatal.

In June 1947, when I finished high school, I went home to Hong Kong triumphantly, diploma in hand. Another decision had to be made as to where I would continue my education.

After being accepted by a couple of universities in Beijing and Tienjin, I was waiting to go north in the Fall. I did not apply to the government-sponsored Hong Kong University in Hong Kong, the only university that existed at the time, because, for one thing, I could not have passed the entrance examination, given in English. Secondly, that university accepted only graduates from government sponsored high schools, and I had graduated from a Chinese high school in China.

The summer of 1947 in Hong Kong was a happy one for me. I was with my family, bathed in luxury. My father had reestablished his taxicab business, and it was doing well. Several of my school friends were also home in Hong Kong for the summer. We had many memorable outings together, going to movies, shopping and combing the many beautiful beaches there.

Waifong had married an American Chinese and went to live in California. American Chinese men in the United States, expected by tradition to marry Chinese women and thwarted by the limited availability of them in America, often came back to China or Hong Kong to find a bride. After the Second World War, with the GI bill and the abolition of the infamous Chinese Exclusion Act, Chinese were able to bring their brides back to the United States. Many Chinese-American veterans were taking advantage of this opportunity. Waifong's husband, a Second World War veteran, had been recommended by an old friend of my father, a man from a well-known family, who had recommended his brother-in-law to come back to marry one of my father's daughters. Waifong decided to be married to this GI after a week. Even though the two young people had known each other only a short time, my parents thought it appropriate for them to be married.

Marriage brokers also found a Chinese American for Waijin and she, too, left Hong Kong for the United States (this marriage was annulled shortly after she arrived in his hometown of Napa, California). For some reason, my mother thought I was too young to be married. Since I had always been a good student and loved scholarship, she was determined that I should get a university education, in part to fulfill her own dream of having an education. So when marriage brokers came inquiring about me, she demurred, hoping that I could continue to pursue higher education.

However, when September 1947 came and my schoolmates

went north to start college, I was not among them. By then, the Communists had come very close to Beijing and Tienjin. War with the Nationalists there was imminent. Because of my leftist leanings and the dangers of civil war, my mother refused to give permission for me to go north to Tienjin to Nan-kia University; instead, she insisted that Waifong, now living in the United States, should find me a school near her in Stockton, California. Obediently, I began the application process, getting transcripts and recommendations, to enroll in Stockton Junior College for the Spring Semester. No one seemed to worry about the difficulties I would encounter should I be admitted into this American college. Everyone thought I could handle it as I had always done. As far as I was concerned, I was just applying to another school to further my education. I had done that a few times before. Somehow, I never really grasped that there would be language problems for me in America.

In the Fall, while waiting for acceptance from the United States, I took classes in the French Convent School, a government-sponsored institution run by European nuns. For the first time, I, born a British subject in a colony of the British Crown, experienced "colonial education." I remember the arguments I had with the foreign nuns and how they unrelentingly chided me for infractions in front of the whole class. I had never been so humiliated in my whole life. My knowledge of the Catholic religion was limited, and religion was a constant source of conflict between the good nuns and myself. Moreover, they expected total submission, no questioning, no argument, and no creative thinking. I don't remember learning anything of significance in the convent school except religious dogma with the Bible as our major source of study. The situation was extremely difficult for a curious, questioning nonbeliever, for I knew there were other points of view.

In December 1947, I received word that I had been admitted to the Spring Semester in Stockton College in California, starting in February. I immediately booked passage for the crossing on the *SS General Gordon,* a journey that would take more than three weeks. With no time to wait for an official passport, I had to make do with only the Certificate to Travel issued by the Hong Kong government.

Once again I embarked on my adventure in education, this time, across the seas to another continent, to another unknown place. Little did I realize that the environment I entered would be culturally different and strange to me, and that it would truly transform me and change my basic beliefs totally.

Before I set sail on New Years Eve, 1947, I heard my mother talking as if to herself: "In a few years, my whole family will be speaking English." I detected a trace of pride as she uttered these words, and I was suddenly aware of what it meant to her, that finally, her family would be able to speak the language of the conqueror.

· 11 ·

A New Start

Afoot and lighthearted I take to the open road,
Healthy, free, the world before me,
The long brown path before me leading wherever I choose.
— Walt Whitman

On a mild January day in 1948, the passenger ship *General Gordon* docked in San Francisco after a regular, slow and uneventful Pacific crossing from Hong Kong. Among the excited passengers standing on deck waving their hands was a bewildered teenage girl arriving in the United States of America for the first time.

After I spotted my sister Waifong and her husband among the welcoming people on shore, I was even more excited and kept waving and yelling, jumping up and down, making sure they could see me on deck. I had finally come to the United States, this promised land, this paradise, my new adventure. My sister was there to meet me.

As I started to survey my new, exciting surroundings, suddenly, to my horror, I realized that I could not read any of the signs or billboards on shore. That had never happened before.

I had gone away from my Hong Kong home to school at the age of twelve, to boarding school in the interior of China. In three and a half years I went to four different schools in different cities. Being away from home was not a new or traumatic experience for me. When I left Hong Kong for San Francisco on New Year's Eve 1947, I thought I was just going to another city to continue my education, to start in a new school. The fact that I was coming to the United States of America made it so much more attractive. Hollywood movies had shown how beautiful and how modern the country was. The people were portrayed as glamorous and fun loving. I was familiar with the kind of lives lead by movie stars like Bette Davis, Lena Turner and Gregory Peck. I had an idea of how these people lived and played from movie magazines. This was a dream come true: I was finally coming to the most advanced society to be educated.

During the three-week voyage across the Pacific, even though I was traveling alone, I had no trouble finding Chinese companions who were from Hong Kong and spoke my language. During those post-World War II years, many young students came to America to study. Aboard ship, these young people had time to get to know each other and created new friendships. An organization of Chinese Students in America Association was formed and several meetings were held during the crossing. It was great fun and the group bolstered my belief that America was indeed an exciting place to be.

Even though the stewards and personnel aboard ship did not speak Chinese, I had little trouble communicating with them because there was always somebody around to translate for me. In China, for the traveler, not speaking the local dialect was not unusual. There were many different dialects spoken in China. Through the ages, because of the lack of transportation, different dialects developed in little enclaves. Often neighboring villagers spoke different dialects to the point that they could not understand each other. I had not been disturbed at all by not being able to speak the language, and I was able to read some of the simple signs aboard ship.

But when I stood on deck that afternoon watching our ship move closer and closer to San Francisco, I realized I could not read or understand many of the signs ashore. Advertising billboards with pretty faces or big cars on them carried messages I could neither read nor comprehend. That was serious. My three years of high school English were not enough to render me fluent in this difficult language. My vocabulary was very limited. There were words I had never seen, whose meanings I could not begin to guess.

In China, since there was only one written language — only the pronunciation of the words was different in each dialect; the written character was the same. I had always been able to read what was written on billboards and street signs, even if I had not been able to pronounce the words in the local dialect. But now, here in this beautiful dreamland, I had become illiterate. Apprehensive and bewildered, I had difficulty accepting what was happening.

Looking at the familiar and happy faces of my second older sister Waifong and her husband, who had come from Stockton, California to meet me, I felt a little easier. After all, I was not alone in this strange land of dreams. There stood family ready to help.

As passengers stood in line to go through debarkation procedures, I was interviewed by an immigration official who could not understand why I did not have an official passport, only a Certificate for Travel. All I could tell the interpreter was that I had to leave Hong Kong in a hurry so I could catch the opening of school for the Spring Semester. There was no time to wait for an official passport. The document I was carrying, a sort of a temporary passport, should be sufficient to show who

I was and where I was born. This idea of a passport was an entirely new concept to me. In all my travels into China, I had never had a passport. One just told officials where one wanted to go and that was enough if one could arrange transportation. Transportation was the most important thing. Besides, America had issued me a visa permitting me to come as a student. Wasn't that enough to let me go ashore?

After much discussion and consultation, the immigration officials decided that I could not go with my sister who was waiting on shore. I did not even have a chance to speak to her. They told me to get into a bus with about a dozen or so people. We were told that the bus would take us to the headquarters of the Immigration and Naturalization Service on Samson Street in San Francisco for further investigation.

This was shattering news. Not being able to meet my sister and her husband was most disappointing, and now, I was to be lead away by immigration officials. Obviously I was on my way to be locked up. I began to recall the horror stories of Chinese immigrants to America as I sat in the bus on my way to the INS office.

Ever since I was a child, I had heard tales about people coming to the Gold Mountain, the name the Chinese gave San Francisco, referring to the Gold Rush of 1848 in California. Since the news of discovery of gold was announced around the world, many Chinese from the Pearl River Delta (including the Four Counties and Far Yuen in Southern China, where my grandparents were born) had emigrated to the United States. They came first as gold miners, then as laundry men, coolies, shopkeepers and as workers on the transcontinental railway in the 1860s. Even though life was hard and lonely here, it was still better than the floods, famines and political tumult they had to endure regularly in China. Through hard work and tenacity, they became successful. Many more would come. Besides sending money home to support their families, these immigrants also tried to bring their neighbors and relatives to America, some legally and some illegally.

The increased presence of the Chinese, their economic success, and their strange customs and appearance had antagonized the American populace so much that tension mounted from the very beginning. Such habits as using chopsticks to eat instead of forks and knives, seemed unusual to Americans. The men in the Qing Dynasty (1644-1911) traditionally wore their hair in a queue; with their pajama-type trousers and jackets, they appeared extremely strange. These men also tended to live in groups speaking their own dialects, not learning any English. Some continued to indulge in the vices of their homeland, gambling and smoking opium, making Chinatown a crime-ridden area. In trying to stop the men from taking jobs from regular Americans, some resorted to violence. Fights broke out in different parts of the United States regularly against these men. These increased anti-Chinese sentiments eventually cumulated in Congress passing the Exclusion law of 1882.

After that date, it was practically impossible for Chinese to come to America legally. But the dispossessed in China still longed to come, so they invented different means. Legally, they could still come as offspring of Chinese men that had become United States citizens. Quite often, people took on the names of these United States citizens so they could qualify to enter the country. Frequently, large amounts of money changed hands for this privilege. For a long time, Chinatown was full of people with a "paper name," the name they took when they bought their "paper," thus the right, from United States citizens to come. The immigration officers soon caught on to the scheme and started to question new immigrants in detail about surroundings in their village and compared their answers with the deposition of the United States citizen who was sponsoring them, hoping to disprove their legitimacy. This process would take months, sometimes years. The newcomers were locked up in barracks on Angel Island in the middle of San Francisco Bay, waiting to be interrogated. Because the Chinese government was inept and ignorant about human rights, there was no recourse whether these people were guilty or not. Every Chinese immigrant then entering America would be locked up and considered guilty until proven innocent, when he could then enter the United States. While waiting to be interrogated, the immigrant would study a book of so called "testimonies" written for him by his sponsor to prepare him for the moment when he was questioned by the INS officer, so that, he hoped, his story would match that of his sponsor. He would be asked such questions as how many windows there were in the house he was born in, or what direction the kitchen in the house faced. The new immigrants, offspring of United States citizens, were treated like prisoners, not allowed any visitors. There are still traces of poems written on the walls of buildings on Angel Island today, testifying to the immigrants' frustration and loneliness as they waited. As a child, I heard many stories of my father's relatives from the village going through these ordeals.

For more than half a century, that was the only way for the Chinese to immigrate to the United States. After the Second World War, however, because China had fought on the side of the Allies who won the War, sentiments in the United States changed about the Chinese. The Chinese-Americans who had served in World War II were allowed to bring in their brides without waiting for an opening in the over-subscribed Chinese quota, which at the time was a little over one hundred persons per year. It also became fashionable for Chinese students to come to study in the universities on a student visa. The postwar United States welcomed them. These new visitors could come legally as students or brides of United States soldiers who fought in the War. However, the quotas for Chinese immigrants still remained the same low number of one hundred and nine a year.

Recalling the horror stories about the early Chinese immigrants as I rode in the bus, I was unhappily reminded that this was not friendly territory. I did not have any "testimonies" to study nor did I apply to enter this country as a United States citizen's offspring, but I knew I was about to be incarcerated. There seemed to be nothing I could do. My only solace was that I knew I had done nothing wrong.

We drove along the water front. I was busy looking at the broad boulevard of the city, its clear blue sky and the sparse traffic and pedestrians. Unlike the waterfront in Hong Kong, there were no tenement houses of the colonial style lining the frontage street. Absent were the covered sidewalks along the storefronts and apartments above them. The old, four-story cement block buildings that were a trade mark of Hong Kong's waterfront were here replaced by rows and rows of single-story warehouses. Because of the absence of hordes of people, vast spaces appeared in front of me. There seemed to be miles between the water on my right and the low hill on my left. I could see the parallel, neat streets headed straight up the hill, block after block. For someone who had grown up in crowded Hong Kong, this was a most refreshing sight; there was room to breathe.

Soon we arrived at the INS office. Six of us Chinese women were taken to an upper floor by elevator to a large dormitory-style room where single beds were lined up in rows on each side. Our belongings were delivered to the front of the room.

We were told that this would be our residence until our cases were decided. Meals would be provided for us in the cafeteria, and the bathrooms were located at the far end of the big room. We had to stay in this room. The doors to the corridor would be locked until meal time, then someone would come to take us to the cafeteria.

Some of the ladies asked the interpreter questions, like how long we were to remain there, or what do we have to do to get out. They were given simple, curt answers such as "I don't know," or "We will have to see." A couple of older ladies started to cry. I was frustrated by this strange reception but resigned to wait it out. I had no idea what was going on, for no one told me why I was being locked up. There really was not much I could do. Coming from a traditional society rather than a legal society, I did not know that I had legal rights, least of all my rights to counsel. All I could do, I told myself, was wait and see what was demanded of me; then, perhaps, I could solve my problems. The faith that somehow, something could be done if we knew what the problem was, had sustained me and gave me what others called courage. I just had to see what developed.

Our days were spent telling each other about ourselves. Most of the ladies were returning residents who had questionable "papers." (There was not one student.) One lady, I remembered, was said to have some kind of criminal record. I later learned that she was thought to have been a prostitute. She was most friendly to me, telling me that she had two daughters my age living in Chinatown. From our windows, she could tell me the names of the streets stretched up the hill from the financial district to Nob Hill. That was Grant Avenue, next was Stockton, and coming down perpendicular toward us was Jackson. The beautiful sight of the neat, parallel streets in a grid lighting up at dusk has stayed with me till this day. Surely, this must be paradise, if only I were free to explore it. During all this time, none of us had any visitors.

One day, after I was there for about five days, a middle-aged, tall, slim Caucasian man came into the room and called my name. He told me to put on my hat and coat because we had to go outside. I remember telling him that I didn't wear a hat. He reassured me that it was all right. After we went downstairs, he introduced me to a Chinese man, Mr. Chow, and said that I could go with him.

"We are going to the British Consulate," Mr. Chow told me, "we will need photos. Do you have any with you?"

As instructed by my efficient mother, I had carried some extra passport photos in my purse just in case there was such need. These I put in his hands. Together we walked around the corner from Samson Street into another building and rode up the elevator to the British Consulate. Mr. Chow didn't say much but went about his business while I waited. Some time later, I signed some documents. Before we left the Consulate, Mr. Chow handed me a new British passport issued in San Francisco on Her Royal Majesty's behalf with my name on it. It was a regular British passport, not a colonial territory one like the ones issued in Hong Kong. He then took me back to the INS building to gather my belongings. We took a taxi to his law office and there my sister Waifong and her husband Walter were waiting. I was free to go home with them to Stockton, to start my adventure in this wonderland with a language and culture totally foreign to me.

· 12 ·

Stockton

"*T*his lower deck is for trucks and the Key System railcars. A passenger car would cross on the upper deck," my brother-in-law Walter explained as he drove across the Oakland Bay Bridge from San Francisco. The three of us were sitting in the cab of his small truck, my sister Waifong in the middle and I on the right side.

I had never seen a massive bridge like this before, and it didn't matter whether we were on the upper deck or the lower deck. Marveling at the steel frame of the bridge, I was busy taking in the view on both sides between the steel girders rapidly passing before my eyes. In the dazzling California sun, white sails and colorful spinnakers glided smoothly on the sparkling bay water as tugboats guided huge ships toward their destinations. The cities of Oakland and San Francisco shimmered at the ends of this spectacular bridge. The truck raced across the steel structure at a speed faster than I had ever experienced; I felt like a soaring bird above the San Francisco Bay.

Walter and Waifong were happy to see me and told me that they had engaged a well-known Chinese immigration attorney to bail me out, after they missed me at the pier. The Immigration and Naturalization Service wanted an official passport, so the attorney asked the British Consulate to issue me one. Fortunately, I had my birth certificate from Hong Kong with me, and the Consul agreed. We were all very happy that I did not have to be incarcerated in the INS building for long.

While I was full of inquiries about this new land of America, Waifong was full of questions about the family in Hong Kong. She wanted to know if our parents were healthy, what our younger sister Waitong was doing and how each of our five brothers fared. I answered all her questions patiently and fully. She laughed at funny anecdotes I told and cried when I relayed how much we had all missed her presence at home.

I had first met Walter, an American Chinese from California, in 1947 when I came home from Wah Ying for the summer. He was introduced to my family by Bo, a family friend who had come from the same village as my father and had gone to the United States to make his fortune. Through the years, Bo had done well in the supermarket business, and now owned a couple of large stores. As was the custom, he had sent money to buy land and built a modern steel-and-concrete, two-story house in the village. The structure, a symbol of success, showed that he, the local boy, had indeed done well, and he was highly regarded by everyone in the village.

Walter, Bo's brother-in-law, was born in the United States and had served in the Army in the Second World War. After the war, Bo advised him to come back to China to look for a wife, since he was financially independent, working as a butcher. As a veteran, he would be entitled to bring his bride into the United States. Bo told him about a wonderful family in Hong Kong from his village, speaking the same dialect, with four unmarried daughters ranging in age from 11 to 22. Thus encouraged, Walter, bearing an introduction from Bo to my parents, came to Hong Kong on the specific mission of finding himself a wife.

Walter was a clean-cut, good-looking, pleasant man in his late twenties. He was taller than the average Chinese, about six feet, and when he smiled, his beautiful white front teeth shone. He had the lightheartedness of a man brought up in America, the air of optimism and fun-loving ease that the Chinese nick-named "big-boy" manners. One could not help but take an immediate liking to these American men and trust them implicitly, even as one wondered whether these "big boys" would ever grow up. Walter had no knowledge of written Chinese but could carry on a simple conversation in Cantonese.

My parents had just come back from the interior of China to Hong Kong after the war and were busy reestablishing themselves. When this likable young American-Chinese showed up, my mother was eager to see if her oldest daughter, Waijin, would make friends with him.

My eldest sister Waijin was a beauty. Her skin was pale yellow with a light pink overcast. Her eyes were large and lively. She was quick to smile. Her nose was thin and straight, not the bulbous one that was the family signature. Not surprisingly, considering her delicate features and fetching ways, she had many suitors.

The only problem with Waijin was that she was the oldest daughter, and she carried the authority of this position to an extreme. To me, she seemed always demanding, unreasonable, self-important and authoritarian. Also, unfortunately for her, the family valued and respected scholarship above all else, and she was not a good student. She was just as intelligent as her siblings, but she did not enjoy studying. She inclined more toward fine jewelry, dresses, movie stars and — to my father's displeasure — cosmetics.

At family conversations, she was often ridiculed for being lazy, unscholarly, "with a long waist," as my father put it. As the eldest daughter, she was often given more duties in the family than the other children, yet she was not appreciated or respected for performing these extra duties. That and not being my parent's favorite, as she thought she deserved to be, left her with a bitterness that lasted her whole life.

At the time, she was being pursued by a university classmate of our eldest brother Yingjim. Should my parents give their consent, they would have been married. But my parents were not very happy with the match, thinking that the young man, bright though he was, would not have the ambition to make something of himself. They suggested that Walter go out with Waijin.

Walter decided shortly he would prefer to date me. My parents countered that I was too young to be dated, let alone married. So they thought my second older sister Waifong should go out with him.

Waifong was entirely different from Waijin. She was full of energy, athletic, almost tomboyish. She also had wonderful white teeth and smiled often. Her personality was open, easygoing and happy. She was most agreeable and was known as amicable and companionable among her friends. Her features were wholesome, her disposition sunny, and her conversation sparkling. She had been seeing a young man in Guangzhou by the name of Tim, an earnest, congenial man trying hard to make a life for himself. Since Waifong had moved back to Hong Kong, however, they hardly had seen each other.

Waifong went out with Walter to show him Hong Kong and to get better acquainted. Within a very short time, Walter proposed. I remember the day my mother told me that Waifong was going to marry Walter and go with him to the United States, I was horrified, accusing my mother of deciding too quickly to marry a daughter off, "just like selling a piece of pork." But the young couple seemed to be happy and in love, so I did not argue further.

They got married, booked passage and spent their honeymoon in Honolulu in the famous Royal Hawaiian Hotel. Waifong's letters from the journey were beautiful and reassuring. The family was genuinely pleased. So pleased, in fact, that shortly afterward, when another American-Chinese came back to Hong Kong to look for a wife, my parents married Waijin to him to take back to Napa, California. This man, Tony, was not as good-looking or as pleasant as Walter. However, his parents, like Walter's, did come from the same village as my parents and did speak the same dialect "same sound, same air," as my mother put it. This fact seemed to reassure my parents, even though we knew very little about Tony except that his family had land in Napa and were well established. No one ever suspected that the marriage would not last. After a short time in Napa, however, Waijin quickly annulled the marriage because of mistreatment and soon married another Chinese-American in San Francisco.

Once across the bridge, Walter drove through the Diablo range, passed the beautiful Lodi vineyards, and brought me to their new three-bedroom, two-bath ranch house on 2112 California Street near the edge of Stockton, a few quiet blocks from the busy highway 99. As with most California ranch houses, the small grassy front yard had a concrete path leading to the front door. To the right of the house, protruding next to the picture window of the living room, stood the two-car garage with a wide concrete driveway in front. Entering the front door, I found the kitchen to my left and the living room on my right. Next to the kitchen was the dining room, facing the hallway. Down the hall, the master bedroom and bath were located on the left and two smaller bedrooms, with a bathroom between them, on the right. The large back yard was still waiting to be landscaped.

This typical suburban house was replicated many times over in America to satisfy postwar demands for housing. Best known was Levittown on the East Coast. In the West, thousands and thousands of ranch-style houses extended beyond the center of small towns. The Bay Area also had Daly City, with identical houses built on parallel streets in a brand new city. The building boom provided new and comfortable housing for many families. Any American with a job could buy these homes with very little or no down payment. Interest rates were low, monthly mortgage payments were less than a quarter of a buyer's monthly salary. With the GI Bill in effect, returned veterans were able to own these homes and raise families, borrowing money from the Federal Government. These homes were also quite affordable for construction workers working on them; families moved in as soon as the houses were completed. The American standard of living went up dramatically and was the envy of the world.

When Waifong and Walter first came back to Stockton, they were staying at a large mansion owned by Walter's sister. But as time went on, the arrangement became strained. Waifong wrote home, complaining about life in the United States. She had started working in the butcher shop that Walter owned. This high-energy woman was telling my parents that she had to get up early in the morning, go to the wholesalers to buy meat, and carry merchandise weighing a hundred pounds or more from the shop to the truck. She would then stand on her feet all day to wait on customers, learning all the while how to cut meat. When they finally finished work at the shop, she went back to her in-laws' house and was expected to work in the kitchen. She longed for a place of their own.

My parents were saddened that one of their daughters, brought up and waited on by maids, should be put to such hard work. (Years later, when my father first came to visit and saw Waifong getting down on her knees to clean the bathtub for his bath, he had tears in his eyes as he asked: "Do you have to do that too?" There was no maid to draw his bath for him.) So when Waifong asked for money for a down payment on a house, my parents were happy that they could help. With characteristic flair, Walter and Waifong chose one of the newly completed ranch houses in this development and later also bought a brand-new Oldsmobile Eighty-Eight with money my parents sent.

Waifong led me now to my bedroom with its neat twin bed and colorful gray-and-red plaid bedspread. Above the bed hung a small triangular flag with a large red "Stockton" across it. A small desk with a chair faced the window on one wall, and a dresser with drawers and mirror stood opposite, next to the doorway. An upholstered armchair completed the furnishings for the bright and cheerful room. My sister had spent much time and care to welcome me to her home.

After a couple of days of visiting, I registered for school. Walter drove me to the school campus of Stockton Junior College on the other side of town and found me a counselor. When he left for work, I was left alone with Miss Tavernor, a kind, stocky woman who seemed energetic enough to move the whole world. With a very limited command of English, I answered questions the best I could, as she helped me fill out forms and select courses for the semester. She also introduced me to a gentle older lady, Miss Mormon, who taught English to foreign students. We communicated with a lot of smiles and embraces. It was a difficult time for me, but their helpful, understanding ways reassured me and miraculously carried me through the process.

I had wanted to become a medical doctor, so I took courses

designed for premedical students. We decided that I should take a total of five courses: English for Foreign Students, Zoology, Chemistry, History and College Algebra. Chemistry and Algebra were familiar to me because I had these subjects in high school. All I had to do was to learn the English terms. Zoology was a lot of memorization. Fortunately, I was trained at a very early age to do that. In learning the Chinese Classics in elementary school, I had to memorize page after page of poems and Chinese classics. Memorization seemed natural after a while, time-consuming but not impossible. The professor, Dr. Arnold, also recommended a Chinese premedical student, a returned veteran named Kingdon, to help me study. Every weekend, Kingdon would come to the house for a couple of hours to go over the material for the week and explain to me in Chinese what I could not understand. His help was most valuable and I did quite well in the course.

The English for Foreign Students course helped me learn vocabulary for daily use, and it familiarized me with many American customs. I loved to do the homework, made easy by more memorization.

But history was reading and writing papers. I could not speed-read English as I did Chinese. I could not let go of words. Any word I didn't know, I looked up in the dictionary and wrote down as a new word I must learn. Reading in this slow way, no matter how I labored, I was unable to finish the assignments. At the end of the semester, I was required to turn in a term paper. Even though I had chosen a familiar subject, China's relationship with the United States in the last century, not without tears did I finish that project. That was the only course that I did not do well in. I earned good grades in the other four.

My life in the United States the first few months was busy

and challenging. Every morning Waifong and Walter drove me to school before they went to work, and I took the bus home in the afternoon. After a little rest, I worked on my assignments until dinner. I put in another two or three hours of work after dinner before going to bed. Such a schedule did not seem strenuous, for I had been brought up that way. I felt no need nor desire to "go play" when there was so much work to be done. With no television to distract me, I led a serene life. I had plenty of time to struggle with my new environment and new language.

On weekends, I would take a day off to go shopping or to go with Waifong to San Francisco or nearby towns for sightseeing. But mostly I worked on my lessons. During that first six months in Stockton, I referred to my English-Chinese dictionary so often that it was worn to tatters. I had to tape the pages together until I received a new one.

And I made new friends. Because Stockton was a small town, the Chinese community learned of my arrival immediately. Many kind people extended their friendship and showed me around. Besides Miss Tavernor and Miss Mormon, I had friends my age at school that I could study with and relax with. Then there was Walter's younger brother, Bobby, who also worked as a butcher at one of the supermarkets. Bobby could not understand why I would come all the way to America just to go to college, instead of marrying him. Conrad, a psychology major, who had a heart of gold, would often come around in the cafeteria at lunchtime to see how I was doing. Katherine, a pretty, vivacious sophomore, invited me to her house and introduced me to her parents and friends. I met the minister of the Chinese Church and was introduced to the congregation, where prayers were said on my behalf. After joining the Chinese Christian Students Association, I participated in many of their activities. Most memorable were two vacations with these young Christians: the first at Zephyr Point at Lake Tahoe one summer, participating in a fellowship conference; the second was a camping trip to Yosemite National Park in April, sleeping under the stars, hiking up Yosemite Falls, swimming in the river, horseback riding, and joining in other favorite activities of Californians. These offered me special rewards for my hard work.

After one semester at my sister's house, I realized that I really needed to learn more English, and the best way to do it was to live among native speakers. I decided, in the fall of 1948, to move into North Hall, a dormitory that was provided for students in the College of The Pacific, a private college that shared the campus with the public Stockton Junior College, a convenient arrangement for all concerned. Both colleges were well run and many students who received the AA degree from the junior college went on to the College of Pacific to complete their Bachelor's degrees.

Dormitory life was natural to me, as boarding school had long been part of my life. Coming from a large family, I had no problem living with other students or getting along with them. Dormitory life in America was no different from what I was used to, and I found people friendly and helpful. My years in college between 1948 and 1950 seem so innocent compared with what I hear about drugs and violence on campuses today.

In the summer of 1948, my younger brother, Yingchou, finished high school in Hong Kong and also came to study at Stockton Junior College. His English was much better than mine since he had graduated from a Jesuit missionary school, where all instruction was carried out in English. He lived with my sister Waifong when I moved onto the campus. He also took premedical courses. We were very focused and studied hard during the two years, feeling we had a mission to succeed. Yingchou reported that at the dockside farewell when he left Hong Kong, our oldest brother Yingjim had told him: "Don't come back until you become a doctor." It was a stern mandate and he took it seriously. He did not go home to Hong Kong until long after he received his medical degree.

· 13 ·

Chicago

*I*n June 1950, both Yingchou and I received our Associate of Arts degrees from Stockton Junior College. We then made plans to go East to finish our undergraduate education. We believed that certain universities on the East Coast were the finest in the country and we wanted to study there.

We had taken great care in applying to the right schools, so that we could make the most of our educational opportunities in the United States. Yingchou wanted to go to Johns Hopkins University, known in Asia as one of the best medical schools. When he had finished high school in Hong Kong, he had applied to the Johns Hopkins Medical School for admission, unaware of the American system in which medical school applicants should already have received a Bachelor's degree. (In the British system, medical schools did not require a bachelor's degree before a student could be admitted.) Johns Hopkins Medical School sent him a letter stating flatly that it was "unnecessary to let you know why" they would not consider his application. This so humiliated him that he vowed that someday, somehow, he would attend that University. Now understanding the system, he had applied to Johns Hopkins University for admission to undergraduate studies as a junior.

We also had applied to McGill University in Montreal, hoping to continue our education in its famous medical school. The world-renowned McGill University, located as it was in a

Commonwealth country, had the advantage of being recognized by the British system in Hong Kong. With medical degrees from McGill University, we would be qualified, without further studies, to take the licensing examination to practice medicine in Hong Kong.

My father did not think it appropriate for women to become physicians. As a compromise, instead of applying to Johns Hopkins University as Yingchou did, I applied for admission to the Pharmacy School at the University of Wisconsin in Madison, Wisconsin, as a backup, thinking a pharmacy career would be less demanding on a woman than medicine. Little did I know that Madison, Wisconsin, as well as Montreal, Canada, had winters colder than anything I could imagine.

We were both flattered and exhilarated when we were accepted by all three schools: I to McGill and Wisconsin, Yingchou to McGill and Johns Hopkins.

That summer of 1950, I took a job as counselor at a Campfire Girls summer camp at Silver Lake in California; Yingchou, with a friend from Shanghai, took a job as a fruit picker in the Central Valley. That was the first employment we ever had. While I enjoyed the beautiful surroundings at camp, learning about American summer camp life, Yingchou was having a difficult time picking fruits under the hot Central Valley sun. He quit before the summer was over.

All the while, even though we had sent in money to hold our places as soon as we received the acceptance letters, we had not decided clearly where to attend. During the whole summer, we debated the pros and cons of each school until the day we bought train tickets to Montreal, Canada. The idea that both of us would be in the same school appealed to us, as did the fact that we could qualify for the Hong Kong licensing examinations when we finished. McGill seemed a more sensible choice. We packed and sent some suitcases on to Montreal at the end of August and embarked on the train journey across the Continent.

At the train station on the day we left Stockton, Waifong and Walter as well as a few friends came to see us off. We were all very sad and crying inconsolably. Waifong was sad to see us go, and we were sad to leave her for unknown territories. Three thousand miles was a long way and we didn't know when we would see each other again. I remembered Walter's sister, Daisy, telling Waifong crossly: "Why are you crying so hard? They are just going away to school." Still, on the California Zephyr, I did not see the magnificent scenery until we were well into Nevada. Tears had blocked my vision.

The train was to stop in Chicago. Waifong had written to her close friend, Tim, who was attending school there. Tim met us at the Chicago train station as arranged and took us to the International House, funded by the Rockefeller family, at the campus of University of Chicago. We would visit Chicago for a few days before going on to Canada.

At dinner that night, Tim asked why we were going to Canada instead of staying in the United States. We told him the reasons.

He then informed us that the Congress of the United States had established a scholarship for Chinese students in this country. The funds came from appropriations that Congress had allocated for reconstruction of China, but could not send now because the Chinese Government had become Communist since 1949. He suggested that we ought to look into it. The scholarship would be awarded to any student who could prove that he was Chinese and could maintain a good grade point average in an accredited college. In any case, he said, since I had been accepted by the University of Wisconsin Pharmacy

School, we should go to Madison to take a look at the campus because it is one of the most beautiful in the country, especially during the summer.

The next morning, Yingchou and I found ourselves at the train station buying tickets to Madison, Wisconsin. We thought we might as well tour the campus since we did have time to spare, neither of us recognizing our subconscious desire to stay in the United States and perhaps qualify for the scholarship.

At Madison, since we had to stay overnight because of train schedules, we first found a room at a hotel near the Capitol building. Then we walked the short distance along State Street to Bascom hill. As we approached the campus, we turned onto a side street and saw a beautiful lake and a big building in front of us, the student union. In the large cafeteria downstairs in the student union, we had lunch on the outside terrace by the lake. After leisurely watching sailboats gliding by in the mild breeze, ducks playing and swimmers frolicking in the warm water, we decided that it was indeed a beautiful place to get an education.

We then walked the long incline up Bascom Hill to the administration building and inquired about registration and housing on campus. The registrar checked and said indeed, they had my name as a new student. The housing department secretary gave us a list of available houses near campus. Dormitories on campus were all filled at this late date, she said, but perhaps some boarding houses near campus would still have rooms left. We took the list and went down Langdon, State, and University streets looking for a room. No vacancies — all available housing was filled. We left the phone number of our hotel and asked the landladies to be sure to let us know if there were any cancellations. At the end of the day, we were exhausted and totally disappointed. There was no room to be found. I could not stay in Madison to attend the beautiful University of Wisconsin. We walked back to the hotel, planning to leave for Chicago in the morning and go on to Montreal.

There was a message at the hotel waiting for us from a house on Langdon Street. We called and learned that there was a place at Langdon Manor — a small room on the third floor and I would have to share it with another girl. Would I mind? We went straight to see it and I congratulated myself that the house was not too far from campus. Suddenly, I was happy that I could stay in Madison and go to Pharmacy School there, one of the best in the country. Perhaps I could even get the scholarship for Chinese students.

That was how my lifelong profession was decided! A room at the inn.

I wrote to McGill University and told them that I was not coming to start school there, would they please forward to Madison the suitcases that I had sent there from California.

I started to prepare for my professional training as a pharmacist.

Yingchou went back to Chicago alone and went on to Baltimore to continue his undergraduate studies at Johns Hopkins University. He had a difficult time there but received his Bachelor's degree from that University in 1952 and proceeded to medical school at Columbia University, receiving his MD degree in June of 1956. We both remained in the United States.

During the first Christmas vacation, we went to New York and visited the Chinese Consulate. After asking whether we were Chinese and looking at our faces to make sure that we were not lying, the Chinese Consul issued us both our Chinese passports from the Republic of China. (On top of my British passport, I received my second passport in this country, before

I eventually received the third one, a United States passport!) With this proof of our Chinese citizenship, we became eligible for the financial aid given to Chinese students. Throughout my stay in Madison, along with about one hundred other Chinese students I received a monthly check from the United States Government, enough to cover expenses. The funds were a generous act of the United States Government, granted in the same spirit as the Marshall Plan. I know of no other government or civilization that would have given as generously as this one. Yingchou and I were both helped toward our excellent college educations.

With this change of plans in Chicago, my direction in life was totally altered. I would no longer study medicine but pharmacy, an entirely different profession, though in my mind at the time these professions were closely related. I would live in the United States instead of living in Canada.

These decisions paralleled in importance my change of plans in not going North to Tianjin for college and completely changed the direction of my life as well as my place of residence. Yet, in my youthful innocence, I took it very lightly. Because of lack of information or experience, we students had little idea what life was about to bring. We had no idea and could hardly imagine the consequences of different decisions, such as the differences of living in the United States or in Canada, for instance. Our decisions about college, made quickly at that time on the basis of a rumor (happily correct), determined the future for Yingchou and me.

I had always thought if one could learn from other people's mistakes in life, it would be much cheaper and easier than learning from one's own life. But like most young adults I often thought of myself as unique, and I thought that the experiences of others would not apply to me. I don't regret the decisions I have made in life, but I surely wish I had had more advice and understood more about the consequences of my choices before I made those decisions.

· 14 ·

Madison

On September 14, 1950, I registered at the University of Wisconsin at Madison as a pharmacy student, and classes started on September 18. In my mind, studying pharmacy was the first step to learn about drugs, Western drugs. Eventually, I planned to study medicine and Eastern drugs, herbal medicine in China, then I could do research and introduce Eastern medicine to the West, following the steps of another Wisconsin graduate, the famous Dr. K. K. Chen, who introduced ephedrine to the Western world. It was a long-term, worthy goal to strive for.

The boarding house I moved into, Langdon Manor at 140 Langdon Street, was about a 20 minutes walk from campus. Even though my small third-floor room felt a little cramped, and I shared a bunk bed with another freshman, the students living in the house were friendly enough and make me feel welcome. I settled in to begin another educational experience.

My roommate was a kind Wisconsin native. It was her first time away from home and she had a hard time adjusting to it. Besides sending her laundry home every week to her mother in a "laundry box," she often went home on weekends. She had a cheerful disposition which helped me greatly to deal with my own homesickness. Even though we had very little in common and often had trouble understanding each other, we still shared many experiences and had a good time doing it.

The cultural shock between us went both ways. I will never forget the day she asked me, "Cynthia, are you Christian?"

I answered lightheartedly, "I guess not, because I was never baptized."

Horrified, she asked, "Have you no morals?"

All I could do to comfort her was to murmur something about my Confucian ethics.

In Lutheran Wisconsin, the heartland of America, it was inconceivable in 1950 that someone was not Christian, no matter where she came from. Fortunately, we never discussed religion or moral standards again, and it was good of her to live with a heathen and not try to convert me! I was thankful not to have to argue with her about theology. She also had trouble imagining the life I had had in China. At one point, she asked whether we had cows in China. I reassured her that we did indeed — cows and many other animals.

For me, the most shocking thing came in the form of weather during the winter of that first year. I had never lived with snow before, and when I decided to come to Madison the weather was not one of my considerations; it did not even enter my provincial mind that the weather in Wisconsin might be different. I was only aware that the Pharmacy School at the University of Wisconsin had the reputation of being the best in the country. When, in the fall, someone showed me a woolen "storm coat" and asked if I had one, I asked in disbelief, "Do you really wear something this thick?" In the eternal spring of Southern China and Northern California, I never had to wear overcoats even in the winter, let alone woolen "storm coats" that were lined with thick fuzzy material. By Thanksgiving, however, I was convinced that I could not survive the year without one of these heavy coats. I also bought boots lined with furry material to wear over my shoes so I could go outside without getting frostbite. The walk up Bascom Hill on campus was good training on how not to fall in snow or on slick ice. One of the standard questions students asked each other once snow started to fall was "Have you fallen yet?" (I have been told that pipes have since been installed on that walk so students no longer face such hazards.) I spent a lot of time in the library studying that year. In the subzero weather, it was a pleasure to be in that warm and quiet space.

My studies were going very well. I loved botany, organic chemistry and pharmacognosy — the plant origin of drugs, and pharmacology — the function of chemicals in the body. It was wonderful to know that digitalis came from the fox-glove plant and that the powerful ephedrine came from Mah Huang, a widely used Chinese herb. However, I was somewhat discouraged to find that, after studying inorganic chemistry, quantitative chemistry, I still did not know much about chemistry. Organic chemistry, biochemistry, physical chemistry and biophysical chemistry were still ahead. Fortunately, I found the entire subject fascinating.

More often than not, news from China occupied my thoughts and dreams during those days. First reports about the Communist government since 1949 were encouraging even though the American press and public sentiment at the time were anti-Communist. My friends in Beijing reported that the universities were reopened after the fighting and that society remained orderly; new government policies were generally for the benefit of the people. It sounded as if the Revolution had been good for China and people were hopeful.

In the fall of 1950, the United States was in the throes of a nationwide Communist scare. The government had no diplomatic relations with "Red China." Congress was trying to pin down "who had lost China," investigating the State

Department, firing the "left wing" workers there. The Republican Senator from Wisconsin, Joseph McCarthy, was conducting his "witch hunt."

Internationally, Communist North Korea invaded South Korea. General MacArthur of the US Army, President Syngman Rhee of South Korea and Chiang Kai-shek of Taiwan were all calling for crossing the Yalu River into China after the UN troops captured the North Korean capital of Pyongyang in October 1950. It seemed that the United States was ready to risk an all-out war to defeat Communism.

Communist China, feeling threatened, responded by sending massive troops across the Yalu River into North Korea from Manchuria in November 1950. From early December on, I was reading the horrors of the Korean War daily: how the Chinese used the "Human Wave" tactic with huge casualties to help North Korea take back Pyongyang from the UN troops; how the GIs kept their machine guns going until they were red hot and still Chinese troops kept coming; how General MacArthur planned to use nuclear weapons across the Yalu River in China to win the War.

Even after President Truman removed MacArthur from his command in April 1951, preferring a non-nuclear settlement instead of the General's belligerent aggression, the war dragged on under General Ridgeway. Well into 1952, I continued to read about Heartbreak Ridge, Pork Chop Hill and other bloody battles in the frozen mountainous landscapes of Korea where human lives seemed to be just weapons in unlimited supply and were of no particular value to anyone.

This tactic of "Human waves" used by China to overwhelm the enemy, plus details of the cruel "class struggles" in China, shook me to my humanist psychic core. My idealistic love for China was based on an inexorable sense of justice for the innocent, suffering people of China. I felt that these good people did not deserve to suffer, century after century. I wanted to find a way to help them, perhaps through education, industrialization, good government or whatever. The Communist ideal seemed, at the time, a way to stop the exploitation of these good people and to grant them a fair share in life. The "Human wave" tactics, in sending large number of human soldiers to overwhelm the enemy regardless of how many would be killed and the Communists' sadistic methods of "struggle" against landlords and "class enemies" offended my basic belief in the sanctity of human life; it turned me against the Chinese Communist government and the whole Communist ideal. I began to realize that this totalitarian government was no better than all the heartless rulers before them. I could not sympathize with their policy of "the end justifies the means." Indeed, I could not love a country with such inhumane policies. I was totally disillusioned.

At the end of 1952, my grades plummeted and I started to lose weight. The house-fellow who oversaw student welfare in the Elizabeth Waters dormitory, where I had moved after the first year, became alarmed. Under questioning, I told her plaintively that I didn't feel like studying, that there was no point in studying, that there was indeed no purpose to life, no meaning in living at all. My lifelong striving for academic excellence to please my mother so she would think me a "good girl" was gone. Pleasing her could no longer bring me happiness. The house-fellow sent me to the university psychiatrist, who diagnosed depression as my problem and put me on the standard stimulant of the day. Nothing helped. I continued in my depressed state, walking around like a lost soul, questioning what life was about, feeling utterly useless, often thinking in circles. Asking my brother Yingchou on the purpose of life brought me the answer: "People don't ask such questions." Discussing it with friends made me feel more like the "odd woman out," for few had the same problems. I had trouble getting up in the morning to go to classes and could not concentrate on my lessons. The weekly psychiatric sessions helped to analyze and pinpoint my problem, but there were no solutions. I realized that I was unhappy because I had lost my purpose in life, my ideal and my country. What could be done about that?

As far back as I could remember, I intended to serve China, be it her Emperor or her teeming millions. It mattered little that I had no actual knowledge of how to carry out this task. I had my goal and I was going to educate myself to that end. Coming to the United States was one way to learn modern medicine in order to help the sick. There had always been a purpose, a goal in my life, however impractical. China needed us, her blessed young and educated scholars, and I, for one, was not going to fail her. How this magnificent dream was formed in my mind was a mystery to me, but I did not find it trivial. I loved China, its culture, its people and its long history; it deserved to be helped. I wanted to do something for it. Now, suddenly, I no longer cherished this dream, I no longer loved China, I could no longer go back to this cruel, Communist-ruled country.

There were more than one hundred Chinese students studying at the University of Wisconsin then. Some were pro Chiang Kai-shek and some were pro-Communist. Because of the anti-Communist climate in the United States at the time, politics was avoided by these students. We had frequent social gatherings, outings and cooking feasts, but not political discussions. I did not find too many sympathetic ears on campus. A few students did go back to China after graduation, and I later learned their unfortunate fate at the hands of the Communist government. These students were branded as United States spies by the Chinese government because the administrators would not or could not believe that the students had come back just to serve their beloved China. Rampant paranoia was found in governments on both sides of the Pacific.

In February 1953, my last semester at Madison, I was invited to move in with two Chinese students, sisters from Shanghai. Hoping that living with Chinese might give me a better sense of belonging, I agreed to join them in a small apartment just off campus. There we could cook our own Chinese food, and perhaps help each other work out problems.

In that small apartment, every day, we went to school and came home in the afternoon, one of us would put on a record of classical music, Tchaikovsky, Beethoven or whatever. Each of us kept busy doing homework, writing applications for jobs or graduate schools, cooking. I remember very little conversation. The two sisters could not understand why I was so devastated by the war in Korea. As to the cruelty going on in Communist China, I should have known about that. That was the way the Communists operated, they had witnessed it in Shanghai before they left. They consoled me that we were in the United States now and should work on getting jobs or entering graduate school instead of wandering aimlessly, grieving for China. I asked what the purpose of life was and they answered that life was for living. One just lived the best one could, taking advantage of circumstances. It was not incumbent upon us to explain life, or to justify it.

This advice did not make sense to me. I maintained that life without a goal or purpose was not worth the effort of living. I could not just live, striving for nothing. In spite of the psychiatric sessions, where every week I went to cry my heart out for fifty minutes and the good doctor tried to help me see through my problems, I remained sadly depressed without improvement. Freudian practices were in vogue and there were few anti-depressive drugs available. Talking did not help.

Realizing the need to qualify for graduation, I finally began to study harder, so my grades went back up to where they had been. I remember taking a course on Beethoven's concertos to meet a liberal arts requirement. Unfortunately, the beauty of the pieces we studied did not rekindle my love for life.

As graduation approached, the Dean and a professor of Pharmacy were concerned about my plans and made inquiries. Like a zombie, I took the advice of Professor Busse, who wrote a laudable recommendation on my behalf, to take the hospital pharmacy internship program of St. Luke's Hospital under the well-known Mrs. Evelyn Grey Scott in Cleveland, Ohio. Again, I didn't consider the weather, only the quality of the program. Dr. Busse assured me that I would be very well trained under Mrs. Scott. By advising me to take this internship so I would qualify for the licensing examination requirements, he not only placed me to learn excellent skills for the job of chief pharmacist in a hospital, but also unwittingly saved me from my total confusion and paralysis at an important crossroad in my life. Without his direction, I would not have been able to find my way after graduation. I am forever grateful for the help he gave me in that critical period in my life. (Half a century later, when the University built a new pharmacy building, I was happy to be able to donate a dispensing laboratory in his honor. He had tears in his eyes when I asked for his permission to dedicate the laboratory in his name. Little did he know that his earlier kindness and concern meant so much in my life.)

Graduation arrived June, 1953. I was finally a trained professional. One more year of internship and a licensing examination and I would be a fully qualified registered pharmacist:

surely an achievement for rejoicing. Yet, I could only cry quietly, feeling extremely lonely and lost. No member of the family came to celebrate with me. The best they could do was to send flowers from Hong Kong and telegrams from different parts of the United States. I don't think any member of my family knew how lost, sad, and confused I was on that memorable day.

That summer, before going to Cleveland to start my internship, I worked temporarily at a hospital in Chicago where second brother Yingchou, who had finished his first year of medical school at Columbia University, had also found a summer extern job in the Cook County Hospital. Friends from Madison came to visit and console me. Schoolmates Fay and Stella came to spend time together with me. We often talked late into the night, each trying to help the other in solving our unique problems in a foreign country. Fay had to decide whether to become a doctoral candidate, which she did, receiving her doctorate degree in biochemistry from the University of Wisconsin three years later. Stella had to decide which man to marry, and she chose a fellow student who won a doctoral degree the year after they married.

Only I remained utterly depressed, not wanting to do anything and just going through the motions of life. Of the three of us, I was the luckiest and most problem-free, for I had finished my studies and had a job waiting for me, but I was incurably, hopelessly unhappy. My former goal of studying Eastern and Western medicine and introducing it to the profession had totally vanished from my mind. My friends simply could not understand why.

As a child, I had lived happily and carefree because I trusted that there were adults taking care of my necessities. There had always been someone there, telling me what to do and what not to do, watching out for me. It was my habit to do as these adults

wanted, following, especially, my mother's commands. Whatever happened, I felt that I would be all right.

Now, all of a sudden, I did not feel that security any more. I
had had the dream of going to college and returning to China
to help, a dream approved by all concerned. Now I had arrived
there: I had graduated from college, I had grown up and was
staring at my future, not just dreaming about it. I was supposed
to take care of myself, my daily living, my needs and my plans
from then on. No one was there to tell me what to do any more.
I was totally free. Yet I did not feel secure. Who was going to
take care of me now? No one. It was an unsettling and lonely
feeling, which, no doubt, fueled my deepening depression.

· 15 ·

Cleveland

*I*n September 1953 , I moved into the nurses' dormitory of St. Luke's Hospital in Shaker Heights, Cleveland, Ohio, one of the neighborhoods in America renowned for its excellent school systems and expensive houses. My room was about six by ten feet with a closet to the right of the entrance and a small window at the far end of the room. Furniture included a twin bed, a writing desk next to it, a chair at the desk, and a Naugahyde-upholstered armchair. Rooms were cleaned and sheets changed every two weeks, meals were served at the hospital cafeteria three times a day. We were issued meal tickets to be marked off for each meal as we went through the cafeteria line. The program provided me with room and board and paid me a stipend of one hundred dollars a month as a pharmacy intern. I was to work for Mrs. Scott five and a half days a week and be trained in the practical aspects of hospital pharmacy.

The Pharmacy department was located in the basement of the hospital. Every day I took the elevator to the basement of the nurses' residence and walked through a long tunnel to the hospital. On the way, I passed the boiler room, Central Supply and Physical Therapy departments, all underground. There was no need to go outside.

Mrs. Scott (we were all professionally addressed as Mrs. or Miss depending on our marital status) was a woman of about fifty with short, graying hair. She was highly intelligent, competent, full of energy and talked with what often seemed a stutter. I later found out that because her thoughts went so fast, her speech could not catch up with it, so she seemed to stutter or even become incoherent at times. Hers was a dominating presence. She demanded your attention by talking constantly, on almost any subject. There was no conversation with Mrs. Scott, one only listened; it was a one-way street. I was told that she last worked in Honolulu years ago before she took up the Chief Pharmacist position at St. Luke's Hospital and that she lived with her mother. Other than that, no one seemed to know anything about Mr. Scott or whether she had any children.

When I started, Mrs. Scott seemed happy to have me as her intern but warned that I had to work hard and not be like the "other young people these days." She ran the pharmacy with an iron hand, and was highly respected by hospital administrators as well as hospital pharmacists around the country. Besides dispensing medication to inpatients and outpatients, St. Luke's made its own lotions, ointments, and other bulk medication for the hospital. On top of that, the sterile solution department made intravenous fluids such as Normal Saline and Glucose 5% for patients in the hospital. This was a very simple task if one knew the techniques of sterilization but it could easily become a serious business should one make any mistakes. Patients could develop high fever if bacteria or pyrogen was present in these solutions. In 1953, the discovery of the effects of pyrogen was still a relatively new knowledge. I remember the stories Mrs. Scott used to tell about how she watched nurses pack ice on the patient's forehead to lower the patient's body temperature as they injected IV solution. They knew that intravenous solutions would cause fever but did not know why. Not until researchers found the culprit, a bacterial byproduct called pyrogen, that caused the fever, could the medical profession take steps to prevent its presence in the solutions. By sterilizing freshly distilled water within a very short time, we prevented bacterial growth and thus the presence of pyrogen in the injections.

Dressed in a white uniform and looking professional, I daily learned new techniques in hospital pharmacy administration, in manufacturing, in methods of control and record-keeping. I was assigned to each department for three months and worked under the supervision of the licensed pharmacist of that department. As I was not yet licensed, everything I did was checked and initialed by me and the pharmacist who checked it. Initials were also clearly marked on every manufacturing step in the record book. All the pharmacists and I had different colored pencils to make check marks on labels as each medication was dispensed or bottled. Everything was checked and double-checked, each step written down, with control numbers assigned to every batch and put on the labels so we could trace every bottle to its origin. I also did research on shelf life and sterile techniques for heat-sensitive and less stable compounds, and presented the paper at the Hospital Pharmacist Convention at the end of the year. In making sterile solutions, I handled all kinds of chemicals and narcotics, routinely making 3% cocaine solution for use as local anesthetic. It was all in my daily routine.

My mother came to visit the United States for the first time that fall of 1953. When I asked for time off to go see her in San Francisco, where she was visiting my sisters, Mrs. Scott shook her head and said: "Your mother can come here instead."

So, sure enough, my mother came to Cleveland and rented an apartment for herself and my younger sister Waitong, who was entering Western Reserve University as a freshman. My mother stayed until snow fell and was delighted with the fluffy white stuff. She had never seen snow in her whole life. Waitong finished that year then transferred to Temple University in Philadelphia to study pharmacy. (She became a registered pharmacist in the United States before going back to Hong Kong to work for the Eli Lilly Company.) My brothers Yingsheung (who was studying in Canada and later transferred to Princeton University, graduating in 1958) and Yingchou came to visit Mother and met Mrs. Scott. They gave her the nickname "demanding woman." I was happy to have family in Cleveland.

A couple of months before my one-year internship was finished, Mrs. Scott needed a pharmacist to work in the sterile solutions department and asked me if I would agree to suspend my internship training indefinitely and work for her as a paid full-time pharmacist. I did not know what it all meant and sought advice from others. The assistant Chief Pharmacist, Miss Job, told me that if I did what Mrs. Scott asked me to do then I would be under her control as to when I might finish my internship. There was the danger, if Mrs. Scott so chose, that I might never finish the internship, and would therefore never be able to qualify for the licensing examination. I followed that advice, declined her offer and finished my internship as scheduled in one year. In the fall of 1954, I took the licensing examination for registered pharmacist for the State of Ohio, and passed it successfully. Mrs. Scott immediately hired me as a full time pharmacist on her staff. I had become a professional woman, financially independent with a well-paying job!

Surprisingly, this would cause big problems for me.

The immigration laws again entered my life. With a student visa, I was allowed to stay in the United States as long as I enrolled for at least twelve units in an accredited school and received passing grades. After graduation, a student was allowed to stay in the country on a student visa for one or two years to gain practical experience. After that, the student was supposed to leave and return to his own country. People on student visas were prohibited from "gainful employment." Now that I had finished my practical experience in the form of an internship and was "gainfully employed" as a registered pharmacist, I had to answer to the immigration office. I could no longer renew my student visa to stay and be "gainfully employed."

As the situation in Hong Kong was becoming more and more dangerous as the civil war between the Communists and the Nationalists spread, my family was of the opinion that we should try to stay in the United States if we could. Earlier, Yingchou had located an immigration lawyer in New York to file applications for me to enter the United States under the Chinese quota. In due time, the ruling came back. I learned that the Chinese quota (only 109 annually) had been oversubscribed to the year 2014. The chances of my being admitted to the United States before that date under the Chinese quota were slim. The lawyer then said since I was born in Hong Kong, she would file applications for me under the Asiatic Triangle Area quota because Hong Kong lies in that area. That quota happened to be still open. Soon, however, this hope too was dashed. Again my application was denied because, the officials stated, even though the quota was not filled, I would still not be qualified to enter the United States on it, because this quota was reserved for people who, "through no fault of their own, could not qualify for any other quota." Since I was Chinese, I qualified for the Chinese quota and therefore would have to enter under the Chinese quota. I did not know why the fact that I was carrying a British passport did not qualify me as British and allow me to enter the United States under the never fully-filled British quota. I suggested that there was nothing legally stating that I was Chinese, even in my British passport. The lawyer said the burden of proof rested with me to show that I was NOT Chinese, not with the immigration office. To this day, I don't know how one goes about proving that one is not of any race. I was trapped in a "Catch 22."

When Mrs. Scott hired me to be a registered pharmacist, I explained to her all these legal entanglements and told her that I would have trouble with the Immigration Office. Typically, she retorted: "Go see your congressman." I had never heard that before. Could just anyone go see her congressman? Besides, I was not a United States citizen and did not qualify to vote, how could I just "go see my congressman," presumably a powerful politician? She said that it did not matter, as long as I lived in this district, I could go and talk to my congressman. She directed me to make an appointment with Congresswoman Frances Bolton, who represented the Shaker Heights district, and discuss the problem with her. Mrs. Scott was very sure that the Congress of the United States of America could do something to alleviate this dilemma.

At the appointed time, I went to Mrs. Bolton's office in downtown Cleveland and spoke to her administrative assistant, explaining my particular predicament. He said he would report to Mrs. Bolton and see what she could do. I couldn't believe it — he actually took me seriously! I waited hopefully but skeptically for the reply. Why would any politician want to do something for an ordinary non-citizen foreigner? This could never happen in China: I did not have an introduction from anyone, I had no influence or wealth with which to bribe her. As far as I was concerned, the fact that I had an appointment and that her assistant even listened to me was remarkable. I would be most surprised should anything come of the meeting!

A few weeks later, Mrs. Bolton's office called and an aide said that the Congresswoman had introduced a special bill, a special bill in the United States Congress, specifying that Cynthia Wai Ying Wu should become a United States citizen. He stated also that I could take "gainful employment" as well, because I belonged to a profession that was "urgently needed." As long as the hospital could prove that they had tried to hire someone else for the position, such as advertising in the newspaper or at the post office, and if no United States citizen had wanted or qualified for the job, then it meant that I was not taking the job away from any citizen. Instead, I would be doing something for the country that no other person could or would do. The Immigration Office would let me stay in the country and work as long as the bill was in Congress; I did not even have to wait till the bill passed before I started work. Mrs. Scott was willing to sponsor me to fill their need, and that would solve my problem. I learned firsthand from this episode a remarkable lesson in democracy: politicians do represent the people. I could hardly believe it! I decided then and there that this was the country I wanted to stay and live in. In a democratic society, every citizen counts, not just the influential and the powerful. What a refreshing and attractive concept.

· 16 ·

Adrift

*F*or the next two years, I walked the tunnel every morning to the hospital, where I worked hard for eight hours under the demanding and critical Mrs. Scott, making sterile solutions or dispensing and manufacturing medication, fully aware that any mistakes I made could mean life or death for the patients. At five o'clock, I would walk, tired and lonely, back to my room, rest a little, then return to the hospital through the tunnel for dinner at the cafeteria and again back to my tiny room.

My depression deepened. I had trouble going to sleep, angry over unjustified criticism leveled at me by the faultfinding perfectionist Mrs. Scott, as nothing I did seemed good enough for her. I had no self-esteem; I hated myself.

The outside world often saddened and bewildered me, even beyond Mrs. Scott's unrelenting demands. News from China continued with horrifying tales of the "three class struggles" and "five class struggles" campaigns. My hope and desire to go back to help China was obviously no longer practical. I was deeply depressed. Even though I had never been a religious person, I was so desperate for help during this time that I found myself praying to a god that I knew nothing of, including its existence. I would often pray: "If there is a god, please, please help me, help China, and help mankind to get out of this meaningless madness."

I was close to a breaking point for no reason I could fathom.

During this time I had male friends that were suitors in the old sense of the word, but I did not even notice their intentions. Jim, the most persistent, did not meet my mother's approval because, even though he was born of Cantonese parents as we were, he was brought up in Shanghai. She did not "like" him when she met him during her stay in Cleveland. As much as Jim claimed to love me and to want to protect me, I felt no closeness or understanding between us. His companionship did not alleviate my depression or loneliness. In fact, his persistence that I should love him exerted tremendous pressure on me. I did not know how to handle it. He could not understand why I would not marry him.

As confused and lonely as I felt, I understood that marrying a man I did not love would not be the solution. As a matter of fact, I felt instinctively that marriage would only complicate matters. I kept thinking, "If I don't marry, it's no big deal, but if I marry the wrong man, it would be disastrous." Fortunately, I realized that marriage was not a guaranteed escape for depression or loneliness.

Professionally, I came to Cleveland to be trained as chief pharmacist in a hospital. But by the time I qualified as chief pharmacist in a hospital, I loathed it. Taking Mrs. Scott as the model, I told myself that I would never be like that. If that's what it took to be an efficient, capable chief hospital pharmacist, I would rather be dead. It was not worth all the sacrifice in human terms to be so demanding, exacting and critical.

The question remained, then, what was I going to do with myself? Jim wanted to get married and I wisely retreated from that. I hated my job and abhorred Mrs. Scott's constant criticism. I did not want to go back to China yet did not feel at home in America. There were no longer any dreams to pursue, ideals to realize or convictions to live for. Life was a suffering void. Yet, in a conventional sense, I had every thing going for me: I had a man who claimed to love me, I had my family, I was highly trained and competent in a noble profession that would also give me financial independence. All I had to do was to wait for Congress to pass my bill and I would even be free to leave Mrs. Scott's unreasonable demands. Life was really not so unbearable, yet I was extremely miserable. I did not love anyone or anything. I did not even love myself. How could anyone be happy without love?

In my questing, inexperienced mind, I thought that if I could free myself from Mrs. Scott's unrelenting oppression, I might be happier. Telling myself the worst that could happen was to be sent back to Hong Kong if I left the hospital, I decided Hong Kong was better than working at St. Luke's, being lonely and unhappy. At least I had family in Hong Kong that might be able to help. Anything was better than living alone miserably in that little dormitory room. So, finally, I gave my two weeks notice to Mrs. Scott. On October 5, 1956, I worked my last day at St. Luke's.

The staff gave me a farewell party. When Mrs. Scott gave me her going-away gift, I thanked her politely. "Well," she said, "it's nothing. You will probably throw it away when you find out what it is." The book she gave me was *The Wisdom of America* by Lin Yutan, the well known Chinese scholar. If she felt that it was "nothing," why did she give me the book? Why did she have to say that? That was Mrs. Scott, and that was the reason why when I told people I was leaving St. Luke's, they inevitably said: "I don't blame you."

Earlier, the Chief Pharmacist at the University Hospital of Western Reserve University in Cleveland had told me that if I ever wanted to come back to Cleveland to work, his hospital would be glad to sponsor me as an urgently needed professional. This offer was a nice gesture, giving me assurance that if I did not want to go back to Hong Kong, the University Hospital would hire me and help me with immigration matters: I did not have to work for Mrs. Scott. To my surprise, jobs were often offered me whenever I interviewed in hospital pharmacies. As I went around the country looking for employment, people frequently said, "If you worked for Mrs. Scott for three-plus years, you must be a very good pharmacist." Employment in hospital pharmacy was never a problem for me anywhere — Mrs. Evelyn Gray Scott was respected that much in her profession. As Dr. Busse had promised before I began my internship, Mrs. Scott did give me excellent training, but at what a price!

I decided to visit my sisters Waifong and Waijin in San Francisco, as I had not seen them since I left California in 1950, and Waifong was in the middle of a divorce from her husband.

I found San Francisco as beautiful as ever. The mild winter gave me some relief from the bitter Midwestern cold that I had hated so much. I found a job with the Kaiser Hospital in Redwood City, doing dispensing, but the commute from San Francisco was quite long. People in the hospital introduced me to a pediatrician who lived in San Francisco and suggested that we commute together. Every day, I took a bus from Franklin Street, where I stayed with my sister Waijin, to Market Street and hopped on the streetcar that brought me to the other side of the tunnel near Twin Peaks. There, at exactly 8:15 AM, the good doctor would be waiting in his car and we drove south on Highway 101, to Redwood City. In the evening when we finished working, he dropped me off at Franklin Street before he went home. From this daily commute, we developed a most unusual friendship.

The doctor was a kind and gentle man, a good conversationalist with a fine sense of humor. A devout Catholic and lover of operas, he was born in Philadelphia to a large Italian family. On our commutes, he happily sang arias from *Aida, La Boheme, Tannhauser* and other well known operas. That was my introduction to such beautiful music. We talked about politics, religion, and life in general. Though the commute was long, I found it extremely enjoyable. I had finally found someone to talk with, perhaps to solve this depression, this mystery of my life.

He lived with a roommate. When he invited me to have dinner at his house, his roommate would get quite upset for no apparent reason. I did not understand that his roommate was jealous. In my innocence, I had no concept of such a thing as a homosexual relationship. After I returned to Cleveland, the doctor thanked me for "the happiness" I gave him. He wrote on New Year's Eve, 1956: "The love I gave you was genuine and good. Because it was good, I've decided not to let society destroy it, but shall keep it in my heart and use it as a goodness to make me tolerant of others and ultimately lead me to my end, rather than have society warp it, mutilate, destroy and degrade it, and eventually transform me into one who hates, keeps away from the good and subsequently away from my end and God." The sentiment was very moving but I wondered whether he was talking about his roommate or me. Or could he be thinking about an interracial relationship?

I worked in Redwood City for only a short time. During this period, I read quite a few novels and other books. (When I read John Steinberg's *East of Eden*, I thought he should be awarded the Nobel literary prize. A few years later, he won it. That made me feel good.) I also had a chance to think clearly. In light of the immigration process that had already started in

Cleveland, I decided to return to Cleveland and work at the University Hospital so I would not have to file a new application or have a new bill introduced in Congress by a California congressman, even if that were possible. At the time, there were rumors that new immigration regulations would soon be implemented to accommodate the "urgently needed" professionals, and there were many people with this status, so the wait would probably be a short one. I reluctantly returned to Cleveland and started working at the University Hospital, living with several girls in a nearby apartment.

While I was in San Francisco, Jim called every day to tell me how much he had missed me. I soon found out that he had married a woman he had impregnated. His excuse was that he had to marry her. Then why was he still calling me?

Life did become easier and more bearable, but my depression continued without reason. I stopped going to see psychiatrists. Time passed slowly, but the pressure from the unreasonable demand of my job was off. The hospital was very satisfied with my work. I also paid less attention to the situation in China, realizing there was nothing I could do about it. On November 25, 1957, less than a year after working for the University Hospital, I was admitted as a permanent resident of the United States by virtue of being "a person urgently needed" and received my "green card."

On one cold morning that winter, I put all my belongings in the car and drove alone to Rochester, New York. There I left everything with my brother Yingchou who was taking his two-year internship in medicine at the Strong Memorial Hospital there. I was on my way to visit Hong Kong, going home for the first time in ten years. I had changed a great deal, Hong Kong had changed a great deal, and China was literally unrecognizable. The country had become "Red," and I could not even go visit. This would be a sentimental journey, and I did not have any idea what was in store for me. But I knew that if I didn't like it, I could always come back to this country. I now had my "green card," my profession and, most importantly, financial independence. I was quite free to decide where, in the Eastern or Western world, I wanted to live.

· 17 ·

Hong Kong

After ten long and difficult years, I was finally going "home" to Hong Kong. On the trip, I stopped over at Hawaii and Japan. A former roommate of my brother Yingchou at Johns Hopkins University was stationed with the Army in Honolulu at that time. He and his mother met me at the airport and showed me Pearl Harbor and the cemetery where the American dead in the Second World War were buried. I could never forget the rows and rows of white crosses planted as far as the eye could see. If men wanted to learn the cost of war, all they had to do was to come here and look. They would find the monuments of human cost in that War. (Unfortunately, the impact was lessened later when the crosses were taken down and replaced by flat tombstones.)

For happier entertainment, they took me to the beautiful Officers' Club high on the hill. The view to downtown Honolulu was an unforgettable sight.

In Japan, I joined a tour to see Tokyo and its magnificent temples and palaces. In 1958, Japan had not yet recovered from the devastation of the Second World War. People were still very poor and struggling. One day, as we were shown the grounds of a temple, I saw a row of disabled veterans begging at the long entranceway. An American lady in our tour went down the line and gave each man some American money. "How could you do that?" I asked her, knowing from our conversation that she lost two husbands during the War and still remained a widow. She told me that she had no animosity toward these men and that had her husbands been alive, they would have wanted her to do the same. It was a hard lesson in forgiveness for me. I had not been able to forgive the Japanese for their aggression and atrocities in Asia, and could not even talk to a Japanese student when I found out that he had been in Nan-king during the War — surely, I thought, he had taken part in the Nan-king Massacre. Americans are such generous souls.

I found Japan a beautiful country with its simple gardens and classic architecture. The people seemed so polite and deferential, it was hard for me to understand why they were such cruel aggressors.

At Hong Kong airport my family greeted me. It was a joyous occasion, and everyone started talking at once. As the car went into the auto-ferry and crossed the harbor from Kowloon to Hong Kong Island, I stood on the bow of the boat watching the skyscrapers and neon signs in Hong Kong. I could not believe what I was seeing: Hong Kong had grown from a small seaport on the edge of the continent into a metropolis, an international trading post in a mere decade.

When China became Communist in 1949, many refugees and their money flowed into Hong Kong,and the colony had benefited tremendously from these escaped resources. The British government skillfully managed its policies and dealings with China, recognized the Communist government immediately while the international community hesitated. Business was booming, high-rise buildings went up everywhere, and new factories sprang up all over the New Territories. The city was making an unmistakable statement about capitalism on the edge of Communism.

Hong Kong was able to absorb the influx of refugees with

ingenuity and new policies. The government's main advantage was its laissez-faire policy, letting the free market take its own course. As long as there was demand, the enterprising people of Hong Kong would find a way to fill it and make money. Wisely, the government also strove to maintain strict law and order, severely punishing any political provocateurs and criminals, staying on friendly terms with Communist China yet not letting Communist China influence its own free capitalist policies. With a flat tax of 12.5% at the time, and the frequent auctioning of government land for development, the government collected enough revenues to build low-cost housing for the poor and the refugees. With an ample supply of cheap labor, plenty of capital and expertise brought from Shanghai and other metropolises of China, Hong Kong was a heaven for entrepreneurs.

Encouraged by banks and overseas markets, Hong Kong could hardly contain itself in its phenomenal growth. Small cottage industries like silk and plastic flower-making turned into multi-million-dollar businesses. Textile and clothing manufacturers were employing every available worker to meet orders from overseas. Domestic servants were becoming harder and harder to find. The construction industry hired able-bodied refugees, legal or illegal, trained or untrained, as soon as they arrived in the Territory. Living standards were on the rise and everyone was taking advantage of the unfettered growth.

In the meantime, Communist China, under the dictatorship of Mao Zedong, was launching one campaign after another to rid the country of "class enemies" and "counterrevolutionaries." True to the methods by which the Communist Party rules, these were large-scale crusades to terrorize the populace and to ensure continuity of the Party's ruling position. In the spring of 1956, Mao called for the "Hundred Flowers" campaign, deriving the name from the Chinese phrase "let a hundred flowers bloom," meaning that everyone could state his opinions. While the Party nationalized industry and commerce and sped up collective farming, the country was enjoying some relaxation of mind control. Mao actually solicited criticism from intellectuals. Many thought that the Communist Party was going to liberalize and might even become democratic; few knew of private remarks Mao made about "enticing the snakes out of the lair." By June 1957, Mao had launched the "Anti-rightist" campaign. When that campaign was over, more than half a million intellectuals were labeled "rightists," humiliated and relieved of their jobs. Some were sent to the countryside to do hard labor. They and their families were forever branded as undesirables, less than human. That campaign silenced China; no one dared to voice an opinion. This would not be the last time Mao terrorized the people. Those who had the courage would risk their lives to escape to Hong Kong, rather than living in fear in China.

Yet, still more foolhardy policies were put in place. In 1958, China launched the "Great Leap Forward" campaign and mobilized the whole country to build backyard furnaces to make steel from anything metal, including pots and pans. The Party intended to double its steel production in these "backyard furnaces." Thousands of farming families were also formed into communes. Production in the countryside plummeted. These wide-eyed economic policies caused a famine in which, it was estimated, over thirty million people perished by 1961. The spectacle of all the Chinese working like ants to fuel their backyard furnaces 24 hours a day to make steel, or moving earth endlessly to build dams, roads, or canals left me incredulous. I could not believe that leaders of one billion people could be so ignorant and simplistic.

I watched these developments with great pain. Political reality had finally cured me of my illusions about serving China. Under the enormous power of a merciless, vengeful, cruel and egomaniacal ruler, many idealists who went through the Revolution enduring uncountable hardships stood by helplessly, watching their precious, lifelong dreams turned into nightmares. Whatever illusions I had concerning China were totally destroyed by the stark madness going on there. And the inability of anyone to stop it drove home a political lesson: power is the all-important ingredient in any political struggle.

My family had done well in the postwar boom of Hong Kong. Besides running taxicab companies, my hardworking father had also expanded his business into real estate development. He had also bought a piece of land in Happy Valley, in a good area of town near the race course, and built a large two-story home for his family. Eldest brother, Yingjim, had married and started a family. He and his wife dutifully lived with my parents, as tradition dictated, in the new house. Trained as a mechanical engineer, Yingjim had gone into air-conditioning manufacturing and cold-storage. Both of these were good businesses during economic expansion.

Third brother Yingsheung had finished college and come home in 1958. Unlike the rest of us, who had been educated in the United States and sought to stay, he had come home to go into the family business. Eventually, his land-development company took full advantage of Hong Kong's increasing population and built numerous high-rise buildings to house them.

I remembered that when he was about to graduate from Princeton University, he planned to take the very first flight home to Hong Kong. I had asked him why. At the time, Hong Kong was not very secure: Communist China could invade it anytime and the territory was hardly able to defend itself. Most of us opted to stay in the United States. He told me he wanted to make some money and Hong Kong was the place to do it. There, bankers knew him and our family well — unlike in the United States, where he would just be a college graduate, without any family support. Also, Hong Kong at the time needed housing for the large number of refugees from China. He intended to build, as he was trained as a civil engineer and interested in housing development. He saw opportunities aplenty in Hong Kong.

As to the question of possible Communist invasion, he was convinced that Great Britain had handled it right by immediately recognizing China so the two countries could have diplomatic relations to work out any problems amicably, while the United States had delayed normal diplomatic relationship with her.

He saw that the revolutionary Communist government had an immediate and enormous problem of administering a billion people in a large undeveloped country and therefore would probably not invade Hong Kong immediately, so as to avoid any military involvement with Great Britain. Strategically, Hong Kong would also serve China as a window for her closed society to the outside world, as well as providing some needed supplies to rebuild the war-torn country.

Yingsheung was sure that China would not invade Hong Kong for a good while, therefore he could go back and take advantage of the opportunity to make some money. I asked him how much money he wanted to make.

"One million dollars," he said.

(Years later when I came home to celebrate my father's sixtieth birthday, I was curious and inquired if he had succeeded. With his characteristic sense of humor, he replied: "No. We weren't successful. We made several millions instead.")

Hong Kong

Hong Kong was indeed stable, growing rapidly and very prosperous. Yingsheung saw the potential of the developing economy and was convinced of the stability of Hong Kong, even though it sat on the edge of a Communist country. His vision and courage have made him an extremely successful businessman. (He has since built numerous buildings, power plants and infrastructure for Hong Kong, China, the Philippines, and other Southeast Asia countries. His hardworking habits, steadfastness, energy, and extraordinary vision continue to astound me to this day.)

I stayed in Hong Kong for most of 1958, taking my qualifying examination to register as a pharmacist in the Colony, working as a relief pharmacist at times, and also helping my family in business while my father and Yingsheung went on vacation to tour Europe and the World's Fair in Seattle in the fall. I kept my mother company, wallowed in luxury, enjoyed being waited on by servants and chauffeurs, and got to know the family again. My mother was very happy and proud to have her educated professional daughter back and wished that I would settle and marry in Hong Kong. Through various transparent social activities aimed at introducing young people of desirable families to each other, I met many nice young men, some educated in the United States. But wedding bells did not ring for me. By the end of 1958, I was ready to come back to the United States.

As a woman, I was not finding many opportunities and I felt restrained and subjected to prejudice, being constantly reminded of things I should or could not do. I also felt uncomfortable with the pragmatic, mercenary ways of Hong Kong. Money was the common denominator of everything. One was too often judged by one's wealth instead of one's character.

After living in the United States, I also found it difficult to live with the judgmental concerns and criticism so pervasive in Chinese society. People took my business as their business and ceaselessly gave me their opinions as to what I should do, whether or not I ever asked for their advice.

One day, instead of using the chauffeur or taxi, I took the tramway home to Happy Valley from the Central district because I liked to sit in the upper deck to watch the city sights. When I arrived home, my mother asked: "Why did you take the tramway?"

"How do you know?" I asked.

"Mrs. Lee called and commented on your frugality. She saw you boarding the tram in Central," was her answer.

I was absolutely flabbergasted that anyone would care to gossip about such an inconsequential act.

All these Chinese customs so familiar to me, which I had grown up with, suddenly seemed strange and unbearable. I was reluctant to conform to these standards of society, least of all to the rules of conduct these petty gossips imposed on me. A decade of living in American society had taught me the values of privacy and individual freedom.

When I first arrived in the United State, I learned that "life, liberty and the pursuit of happiness" were "unalienable rights," for everyone. I was shocked thinking that this must be a very selfish society to give its citizens the right to pursue their "personal happiness," not society or anyone else's happiness but just his individual happiness. In my obligations-oriented upbringing, this was not allowed. One must discharge his duties to everyone else first before one could think about his own individual well-being. Then, as I lived in the United States longer and longer, grew more and more accustomed to the idea, saw the results of its practice and experienced its wonderful effects, I loved it. Personal happiness became as important to me as life and liberty; for without happiness, life and liberty did not mean much.

Happiness might mean different things to different people (if one is allowed enough freedom to interpret it), but whatever it is, one has the right to pursue it. It is a beautiful concept. Not only that one is entitled to be happy but one possesses the right, freely, to find ways to be happy. The ways to find happiness could be different for each person, but one has the right to find his own way to happiness. What ultimate freedom!

Once I had tasted this individual freedom, I found it difficult to think in the old-fashioned way of fulfilling duties and obligations. I longed for the freedom in American society, the value of an individual, the protection of laws for women's rights, the abundance of opportunities and possibilities that are open for everyone. Most of all, I missed the gentleness, friendliness and the non-judgmental, encouraging ways of the American people. It was very clear to me after this visit that I could live neither in Hong Kong nor China unless I sacrificed my personal happiness and freedom, which I was not willing to do.

Even though living in the luxury and care of my family was wonderful and helped me recover from my loneliness and depression somewhat, I did not enjoy living in Hong Kong. In the winter of 1958, I made plans to return to the United States, thoroughly rid of my dreams and ideal of serving China. I was determined to pursue my personal happiness and independence in the land of freedom. I had no idea what that happiness might be or how to go about it, but I was convinced that I could only do it in the United States of America, not in Hong Kong.

· 18 ·

Boston

*Y*oungest brother Yingbun, now 16, had convinced my parents to let him come to the United States to finish high school. Brother Yingchou, who was doing his residency in internal medicine in Boston at the time, was living with him in a small apartment in nearby Brookline. Yingbun had began his study at Brookline High School in the fall of 1958. My mother thought it would be a good thing for me to join them in Boston to keep an eye on "the boys" and to keep house for them. I did not question why I should "keep house for them." Since I had no specific plans to live in any other city, Boston seemed to be an enchanting idea. It is well known as a cultural center of the United States, and I had never lived on the East Coast, so this seemed like a good opportunity.

I returned to the United States and joined them in Brookline. We moved into a two-bedroom apartment on Brookline Avenue. Without much trouble, I found a job at the famous Massachusetts General Hospital as a staff pharmacist. Every day I went to work and came home to cook for my two brothers. We had good friends in the area, our social life was busy and interesting. I settled in and found life peaceful and pleasant, living with family.

Feeling momentarily restless, I began taking an evening course in psychology at the extension school of Harvard University and enjoyed greatly the stimulating experience. I made friends with Harvard students and professors, went to student "hang-outs." The academic world in Boston was exciting: there were lectures, plays, seminars and conferences going on all the time. I was much attracted by the people and the cultural events. Finally, I decided I would go back to school full time. And I wanted to go to Harvard University.

Since Harvard and Radcliffe College were still separately administered for men and women, I went with a friend to the admissions office at Radcliffe College to ask for an application form for graduate school.

The lady at the front desk asked: "Where did you do your undergraduate work?"

"At the University of Wisconsin at Madison, Wisconsin." I told her.

She was not at all impressed: "Competition is very keen here, especially for someone from schools 'out there.'"

"Schools out there!" She did not even see fit to give me an application form. I left the office empty-handed!

It was not in my character to take this kind of brush-off. In fact, this kind of derogatory remark only spurred me to further action. I immediately decided that I would talk to someone at the Medical School to see about getting into a graduate program in Pharmacology.

After making an appointment with the Pharmacology Department at Harvard Medical School, I had an interview with the famous Dr. Otto Klayer, head of the Department and the developer of the heart-lung machine.

In his German-accented English, he kindly asked: "What are you doing now?"

"I am working at the Massachusetts General Hospital."

"Why do you want to come back to school?" He wanted to know.

"The pharmacy job is rather routine and boring. I would like to learn more about actions of drugs in the human body. Perhaps do some research on Chinese herbal medicine, a long-time ambition of mine."

He smiled: "Would you like to work part-time and go to school part-time?"

I shook my head: "If I were to do it," I told him, "I would put my whole heart and soul into it, not just part-time."

He gave me an application form to fill out and said: "We will see what happens."

I left his office, encouraged and full of hope. The kindness of this great man still warms my heart every time I think of him.

I filled out the application, mailed it, requested transcripts from the two colleges I had attended; asked for recommendations from former professors and the chief pharmacist at Massachusetts General Hospital, and waited; hoping against hope that I would be accepted.

At that same time, Yingbun was also applying to Harvard College as a freshman, though he was still one year short of graduating from Brookline High School. He had always been a good student and was the brightest of us all. All his life, he had collected so many accolades that he complained at one point that it was boring to be first all the time. If anyone could get into Harvard, surely, he would be the one. He would be accepted, I told myself, but I wouldn't be.

Yet I teased him: "Wouldn't it be funny if I get into Harvard and you don't?" That did not sit well with him.

One by one, the letters came. His arrived first: he didn't make it. Harvard rejected him and asked him to re-apply when he finished high school.

Then my letter came. Not only was I accepted into the

graduate studies program for biological sciences at Harvard Medical School, I was also awarded a scholarship for the year! It would cover living expenses and tuition. What a great surprise. This would provide me with another wonderful educational opportunity. At age thirty, I was to go back to study for a doctoral degree at prestigious Harvard University! For the first time in my life, instead of rejoicing at an educational opportunity, I was scared.

Yingbun also had applied to and was accepted by the California Institute of Technology in Pasadena, California, as a freshman. He decided to go to California. Second brother Yingchou had finished his residence in Internal Medicine and had applied for a post-doctoral fellowship at the University of California Medical School at San Francisco. He too was accepted.

In September 1959 they both left for California. A fellow classmate, Helen from St. Louis, moved in to share the two-bedroom apartment with me. I began my studies at Harvard Medical School, within walking distance on Brookline Avenue where I lived.

We attended classes with the one hundred or so medical school students the first year. I was one of only six female students in the combined medical and graduate school class. The first day of class found me staring at numerous Phi Beta Kappa keys hanging from student's tie clips or pocket chains. This was going to be as difficult and competitive as I had feared.

It had been six years since I had done any academic work. I had forgotten my calculus, most of my physics, and a lot more. The biophysical chemistry was explained in mathematical terms that I had never learned. The physical chemistry I had in pharmacy school included only the properties of colloidal solutions, nothing else. My preparation in basic sciences and mathematics were totally inadequate for my studies.

I plowed on and on, tried to catch up and read the most up-to-date research journals, often studied until early hours of the morning. Long hours were also spent in laboratories caring for animals and performing experiments on them, checking results as needed at all hours of the day and night. Taking care of animals proved to be my most difficult task. Not being brought up with animals, I had an innate fear of them, large and small. Once a guinea pig bit my hand when I tried timidly to pick him up and I had to get painful tetanus shots in the clinic. The experience only increased my fear of these little creatures.

For my research project, I had chosen to study the transmission of signals in nerve cells, in neurons and synapses. In order to do that, I should somehow, sometime, study the giant squid inhabiting the warm waters of Florida, for they had the largest neurons. I had no idea how I could wrestle with these octopods and perform precise experiments on them.

It was all unfamiliar and difficult to me. My depression returned and became unbearably painful. I took to alcohol to relieve the pain. Once I had too much rum and became drunk. The dizziness and the unpleasant experience of vomiting taught me that the physical suffering was worse than depression. It stopped my indulgence. My roommate Helen and her medical student boy friend took care of me and told me that I should never chose rum to get drunk.

The depression eventually affected my academic performance, and my adviser thought I should go over to Cambridge, the main campus, to visit the clinic and see a psychiatrist. Again, once a week, I started to talk to a psychiatrist and cried for fifty minutes in each session. The depression did not get any better. I often felt "out of it."

One day, after three months of intense studying, I went downtown to a department store. As I walked around in the huge emporium, I found myself asking: "What am I doing here?" I was totally lost in the racks and racks of beautiful cloth and thought it had nothing to do with me. It all looked so alien. I could not remember why I had gone downtown and did not know why I was there. I found my way out in horror.

That summer, one of the professors offered me a job in his laboratory to help him with the study of liver functions in animals. In order not to disturb the animals excessively and change the body chemistry, we had to kill them quickly. The professor had a small guillotine made specially for that purpose. I spent the summer chopping heads off tiny guinea pigs and taking out their livers immediately for study. That was the last thing I would want to do, ever.

In the fall, I did not register for the second year at Harvard. Instead, I moved out of the Brookline Avenue apartment because I learned from the landlord that my brother Yingchou, who had been paying the rent on the apartment I lived in, had written him stating that the rent would no longer be paid after August of that year. I went to live with friends on Commonwealth Avenue.

I had no home, no job, no goals, nothing to do. I just went through the motions of living, aimlessly, not finding any reasons for it. I had no desire to get up in the morning, did not want to eat or clean myself, did not socialize with people nor did I look for work. There was no demand placed on me. I did not place any demand on myself. Everything was a confusing void. I had no idea what to do with life. I only found it painful to live, carrying on day after day. Eventually, I decided to commit suicide. I thought if my life had no purpose and I was not enjoying it, I might as well do away with it, one always had that option. Any number of barbiturates would do the job quickly and easily.

Trying to figure out what else I had to do to tidy up on earth before I abandoned it, I found that there were several thousand dollars in my bank account. I should have no use for it after I died. What should I do with that? Recalling that Bostonians always talk endlessly about Europe and its Old World splendors, I thought, since I had never seen Europe, why not go see what was there before I died? I imagined that it would be quite different from the United States. Perhaps that would give me a different point of view. I was still curious.

On a stormy day, while Boston was battened down waiting for a hurricane, I went to the Thomas Cook travel office downtown and told them I wanted to go to Europe.

The clerk looked at me. "Where in Europe?"

"Everywhere. And I want to go now."

They finally found space on a "grand tour" of central Europe, traveling by bus for three weeks. I signed up, went back to my friend's house and packed a few belongings, ready to get on the plane. I did not tell anyone in the family where I was going or why. The family did not seem to care anyway. I would just disappear, vanish. I was not important to anyone, there was no need to let anyone know anymore.

That weekend, leaving Boston and the United States was like saying good-bye to the whole world, abandoning it all together. I didn't care about anything.

These feelings of abandonment happened to me every time I traveled. I just "let go." As soon as I got on the plane, I was in another world, anticipating the new things to come that had nothing to do with my past or daily life. It seemed like a brand new life to look forward to. Not letting anyone know my whereabouts would stop friends and family from reaching me and reminding me of the reality of my existence. This was my escape route, my way of "re-creation."

· 19 ·

Grand Tour

*F*ortunately, the Thomas Cook Company had a representative waiting for me in London to guide me
through the airport and onto my connecting flight to Paris.
There I joined the official tour led by an older Englishman who
had worked for Thomas Cook for many years. He showed us
Paris: the Eiffel Tower, Tuileries Gardens, Louvre, Montmartre,
the Left Bank and the Notre Dame Cathedral. It was all new
and dazzling for me.

One night, a group of us took a nightclub tour of the city.
That was a must-see in Paris, they said. At dusk, we boarded the
bus in front of the hotel and started a round of nightclubs. In
the first club, as soon as we sat down, drinks were served.
Someone was singing on stage. A scantily clad woman started
performing sexually provocative acts. The acts were short, and
we stayed only a little while before going on to the next club. As
we went from club to club, the shows became more spectacular
and more daring. That night I saw naked men and women performing the sex act on stage — something I would surely never
see in Boston! After visiting five or six clubs, we ended up at the
Folies Bergères to watch their famous show, gorgeous women
wearing colorful feathers, and other all too-brief coverings. An
eye-opening experience for me indeed.

The three days in Paris visiting the Arche de Triomphe,
churches with gargoyles and flying buttresses, wide boulevards,

numerous museums, classical buildings and grand monuments took my breath away and captured my heart. I had never seen any city as fabulous as this: Again and again during my life, any time I had a chance, I would come back to Paris.

Our tour continued to Brussels, Belgium. There, I saw the magnificent Grand-Place, a small square surrounded by ornate medieval guild houses. These old edifices were stately and beautiful; I much preferred them to the modern buildings. We stayed in Brussels only one night, and went on to the Netherlands. Amsterdam impressed me with its cleanliness and the huge number of bicycles. During rush hour, the streets were clotted with bicycles, not cars. There were few pollution problems there!

From Belgium, we went east to Germany and south along the Rhine River. The bus driver did not take the autobahn, but drove instead on the state and tourist roads. We saw many interesting medieval towns along the way. From the bus, we could also see the vineyards and forests along the river banks. Someone pointed out an island in the Rhine river and said it was Lorelei, "the fabled romantic rock where fair Rhine maidens lolled and often sent sailors to their deaths." I looked and looked, but saw no maidens. "When I get home," I told myself, "I must look up in the dictionary what the word 'romance' means." I later found the definitions in *Webster's Collegiate Dictionary* as " a made up story, usually full of exaggeration or fanciful invention." So much for Rhine maidens and romantic tales. It was all imaginary, "made up stories," and "fanciful inventions."

We arrived in Cologne late at night, ate dinner and went to bed, prepared to see the town in the morning. On the tour of the city the next day, I was shocked. Nothing remained but bombed-out buildings, block after block. They showed how badly damaged Cologne had been. Most of the city was still in ruins fifteen years after the Second World War. In one block, the cathedral stood silently alone, undamaged. We toured the magnificent edifice and were told that pilots of the Allied bombers, when bombing the city, had been instructed not to destroy this monument. A few pilots had lost their lives in the raid, but the majestic cathedral stood unscathed amid blocks and blocks of rubble.

Heidelberg, our next stop, was a medieval university town. It was well preserved and not destroyed in the War. Its castle on the hill typified many of the towns we saw but was by far the most impressive. We also visited Coblenz, Baden Baden and Mainz, then crossed into Austria to Innsbruck. In the nearby village of Oberammergau, the Passion Play was being performed. Some hundreds of years ago the villagers had promised God to put on the Passion Play every decade. The whole village took part in the play, acting out Christ's Passion before Easter. I had no ticket to the performance, but, while walking around the quaint little village, I was startled to find the character of Christ in full costume walking down the hill during intermission. The devotion of the town's people was much in evidence.

Innsbruck was as far east as the tour went. From there we passed through the small kingdom of Liechtenstein to Lucerne in Switzerland. In this small town by Lake Lucerne, I watched mothers pushing strollers by the lakeside, lovers walking slowly and smiling at each other, young children jumping and playing in parks nearby. It was a calm and peaceful Sunday afternoon. Could Switzerland's neutrality in the War have spared its people the pains others suffered in the Second World War? I was quite sure it had.

That night at dinner in a small inn by the lake, a young man came up to me and offered a bunch of edelweiss that he had collected. I was told that this plant grows only in very high altitudes and he had just collected it from his climb. The small blossoms represented great effort. We could not communicate in any language, but I understood his sentiments. I hoped my smile expressed my thanks.

The next day we turned north, back to France. We stopped at the artist colony of Barbizon to have lunch, saw Fontainebleau briefly, and arrived at the Paris airport in time to catch our flight to London.

During our stay in London, whether I was admiring St Paul's church, the Parliament buildings or the British Museum or just walking around at the Strand, I felt quite comfortable. Knowing the language certainly helped a great deal; also, the history and the common heritage between America and England helped me to feel at home in these surroundings. Suddenly I thought, "I could even work here in London if I wanted to — since I have a British passport, therefore no need to apply for a work permit, and my Hong Kong pharmacy license would qualify me to practice here as a pharmacist." I realized how fortunate I had been to have such freedom. Nevertheless, after two days of sightseeing in London, when we left for Boston, I felt good to be going "home."

We had visited France, Belgium, The Netherlands, Germany, Austria, Liechtenstein and England; in all, seven countries. Not the whole of Europe, but grand enough. I saw how different many Europeans lived and felt each country's spirit, understood somewhat their heritage and learned a great deal. I also observed how difficult it was for some older members of our tour to get in and out of the bus or to take the long sightseeing walks. These were hardworking Americans who finally, upon retirement, had a chance to visit Europe in a grand tour.

They seemed to have enjoyed themselves, but their endurance was limited. I told myself that I should not wait until I retired at the age of sixty-five or older to travel, for I might not live that long or might be physically unfit by then. I resolved to take every possible opportunity to go places and to learn about other countries and people. The younger I acquired this knowledge, the longer and better I could benefit from it.

When I landed at Logan Airport in Boston from London, the air was crisp and clear with warm sunshine reminiscent of California. Even though the New England air felt chilly, I came back to the United States with a warm heart, feeling lucky and privileged, happy to be alive. The suicidal thought I had before my European trip now seemed utterly ridiculous. True, I had no home, no dreams, and no bright future as my Harvard classmates probably had, but I still had my profession, my independence and complete freedom. Also, I was educated enough and had enough practical skills to make a good life for myself if I tried. I was on the manic phase.

The friends who hosted me in their apartment welcomed me back with open arms. They told me I could stay as long as I wished. They were happy to share their apartment on Commonwealth Avenue. So there we were, the four of us: Tienfon and his sister, Tienwen (both Harvard graduate students from Taiwan), Tienfon's girl friend Sujen, and me, helping each other to study, work and solve life's problems in a foreign country. They had many friends, fellow students from the Boston area. We often got together to cook Chinese food and we talked endlessly, discussing school, politics, and life in general.

My depression seemed better and I started looking for something to do. The most logical thing was to go back to work as a pharmacist. Through an employment agency, I landed a job with a small, non-profit Catholic hospital in Roxbury. The chief pharmacist there was about to become the head of Purchasing Department, so he needed someone to carry out the day-to-day responsibility in the pharmacy. The work, providing medication for in-patients, was easy and routine. The pay was good and the hours reasonable. I drove to work in the morning and came home in the afternoon, nine to five, regular hours. Life took on a calm normalcy.

After a few weeks, I began to sense that something was wrong. When I checked in merchandise from wholesalers, inevitably some items were missing although the wholesaler said they were sent. When I talked to the purchasing department about them, the chief pharmacist, my boss, always said the items had come in. Yet I never actually knew where they were. If I stated that our pharmacy really needed the items, my boss would bring them to me from somewhere, telling me they were in the storeroom to which I had no key. Every so often the assistant administrator, a good-looking young man, would come into the pharmacy and ask for items that no administrator should need. On my chief's orders, I gave the man whatever he asked for. No records or prescriptions were kept of these items, as any good pharmacy practice would dictate. Soon I realized that these men were stealing from the hospital, and it disgusted me. I did not want or had not the courage to go to the nuns that ran the hospital to report these irregularities. Now, my work became most unpleasant.

I decided to apply for work in different pharmaceutical companies to do research and product development, where perhaps I could use my graduate training. I did not apply to do pharmacology but product development, to avoid working with animals.

After applying to several companies, I had an interview with the Burrows-Wellcome Pharmaceutical Company in

Tuckahoe, New York, a good-sized old company with an impeccable reputation. At the interview, a kindly old gentleman, head of the Research and Development Department, told me about the kind of work they were doing and said that my qualifications were just what they wanted. He patiently listed the compensation package, including generous retirement benefits, and asked if I would join them. That was the first time I had thought of retirement benefits. Working as a hospital pharmacist, I always felt, was my contribution to society and my duty. The hospitals never mentioned retirement benefits. I received compensation only so that I had some means of supporting myself. Accustomed to living life a day at a time, I had no long-term plans. At thirty-one, I never thought about living to a retirement age of sixty or sixty-five. Furthermore, to have an employer paying to support me when I retired was a novel idea, for I always felt retirement should be an individual and personal responsibility. Nevertheless, the whole package sounded good, and I accepted the job. I gave my two-week notice to the hospital in Roxbury — what a relief to get out of that pharmacy!

In the winter of 1960, on a sunny Saturday morning, I packed my belongings into the car, said goodbye to my kind friends in Boston and drove south to Tuckahoe, New York, a pleasant drive on the New York Throughway. I rented a room in a home near the Burrows-Wellcome plant.

My landlady was a widow with grown children. She treated me almost maternally, asking where I had been if I came home late, wanting to meet my friends and asking me detailed questions about them. If I had a phone call from a male voice, she definitely wanted all the information about this person. I began to feel uncomfortably like one of her children. When I told my friends about my relationship with my landlady, they all decided that I really did not need a housemother or a nurse-maid, and they suggested that I live in New York City instead.

I met four Chinese women students from Taiwan living in an apartment on York Avenue and 72nd Street on Manhattan's East side. Now and then, one of the girls would get married and move out of the apartment, and another would move in to take her place. By and by, the place became a gathering center for Chinese foreign students, a kind of home away from home. Chinese students visiting New York inevitably found their way to meet the girls living there. Often, a long-distance romance resulted. (One married a man from Washington State, another married one from Michigan.) That March, one of the girls got married and moved out, and my friend Neinchang asked me to move in. The forty-five minute commute from Manhattan to Tuckahoe was manageable, and I was eager to be out of the in-quisitive widow's house, so I accepted the offer. For the next several months, I worked in Tuckahoe in West Chester County and fulfilled my dream of living in Manhattan, experiencing city life.

In this fascinating metropolis, we spent time in museums, theaters, and movie houses, went shopping and sightseeing, showed visiting friends around the city, and found foodstuffs both familiar and unfamiliar to us. We thoroughly enjoyed the riches and treasures New York City had to offer.

Work was easier than I had expected. My assignment was to study the shelf-life of drugs. The experiments involved put-ting pills and capsules in different colored containers on shelves for varying periods of time, then analyzing the contents to determine if there had been deterioration and how long it had taken for the decline. Often drugs needed to be put on the shelves for a long time, and there was really not much work to do. I spent a lot of time reading journals and studying chemical compositions. Sometimes I hid in the lady's lounge and read novels. During this period, I had a chance to study Aldous Huxley intensely.

Fellow workers were friendly and helpful. One or two had a master's degree or a doctorate, but most were registered pharmacists. One day, I was analyzing a chemical and began chatting with a fellow worker about the United States. The topic of California came up. I mentioned how beautiful Yosemite and Lake Tahoe were and reminisced about the wonderful mild weather in the San Francisco area. He sighed and said he wished he had a California license so he could go there to practice. At that time, California and Florida were the two states that would not reciprocate with others, for fear of too many pharmacists migrating into their states. I had taken the California licensing examination the same year I took my Hong Kong license. I told him casually that I had a California license.

"What are you doing in Tuckahoe?" he asked. "Why aren't you working in California? The pay in California is double what we get here. Also, there's a union out there so pharmacists get good benefits."

He also pointed out that the population in California was growing, so that there was a constant demand for registered pharmacists.

I had not paid much attention to what was happening in California over the years and was unaware of these opportunities. I enjoyed the East Coast, but as winter approached the commute on the New York Throughway became hazardous. Driving in the snow was difficult, and I dreaded it.

In Hong Kong, my father was preparing to celebrate his sixtieth birthday at the beginning of 1962. He had hoped that all his children could come back to celebrate with him. In the Chinese tradition, the sixtieth birthday is a very important event.

In order to show our respect and obedience, we should all go to wish him good health and longevity. He would be most happy to see all his nine children gathered around him.

After much conflicting deliberation, I decided to resign my position at Burrows-Wellcome Company and go back to Hong Kong to celebrate my father's birthday with him. In the back of my mind was the thought that perhaps on my return, I could live and work in California.

By now, New York had become mundane and indeed inconvenient. The winter weather and the commute on dirty streets had become too much of a problem. I had a great desire to get away from it all. Yet, the decision was made with trepidation. I remember feeling lost and empty because I thought I had not accomplished anything since I last visited Hong Kong. I had a deep sense of failure because I had not finished at Harvard. Academic achievement was so important to my life, that I could not forgive myself for squandering that opportunity.

Nevertheless, I gave notice at Burrows-Wellcome, packed all my belongings again into my car, stored them at the widow's garage in Tuckahoe, said goodbye to my roommates and went home to Hong Kong, expecting another long stay.

My journey took a long time. Since I had enjoyed Europe so much and since there were countries I had not visited, I decided to fly around the world. Instead of going west, I flew eastward to Rome, and I booked a two-week bus tour to see Italy and another week to see Spain. Buying a round-the-world ticket to get to Hong Kong became the pattern of my home visits and I eagerly took up travel as a hobby.

· 20 ·

Around the World

I was met in Rome and brought to our hotel near the Spanish Steps to join the tour group of about twenty people, mostly older couples. We stayed in the city for only a couple of days, just long enough to see the standard tourist sights: the Forum, the Appian Way, the Pantheon, the Colosseum; and most impressive, the Vatican, St Peter's and other churches. As I had never studied Western Civilization, the magnificence of Roman architecture surprised me, even though I saw most of the structures only as ruins from long ago.

The size of the Colosseum and the Pantheon and St Peter's especially astonished me in the scope of their undertaking. In St. Peter's Church, as I entered, I saw Michelangelo's Pieta on the right-hand side near the entrance as a small statue. But when I went closer to look at it, I realized it was huge. As I stood in front of the statue, the elegant marble carving with Mary looking down sorrowfully at her lifeless Son loomed large above my head. I began to grasp the size of the church — the distance from the entrance of the church to the statue was so vast that the statue had initially appeared small. The elaborate columns supporting the canopy over St. Peter's tomb by Bernini were splendid. I had to stretch my neck to look up at the ceiling of the Sistine Chapel to see Michelangelo's panels. The variety of architectural styles also made Rome a heaven for me; in every direction, I saw remarkable buildings or ruins in

Etruscan, Classical, Renaissance or Baroque styles. Piazzas, fountains, and winding streets made Rome a most interesting city to walk in, and at every turn I discovered wonderful sculptures, fountains and architectural treasures.

Before I spent time in Italy, I imagined that it was inhabited by tall, good-looking Romans, still dressed in their togas, like the Egyptians in their long robes. I was totally disappointed when I saw only short and swarthy men in modern shabby trousers and shirts. "Serves me right for not studying history," I thought. "If I had learned the history of invasions and occupations by different tribes through the ages in the Italian Peninsula, I would understand the makeup of the Italian people and would not be looking for Romans wrapped in togas."

We were also shown villas built for popes and cardinals and their powerful relatives. Some of the structures were well preserved. The elaborate buildings, gardens, lakes, and secret entertainment grottos showed how lavishly they had lived. These priests were no different from secular rulers in their love for luxury and ostentation.

We headed north from Rome, driving through the beautiful countryside. I was introduced to Orvieto wine in the charming little town of that name. In the hilly town of Siena, I discovered delights and hidden treasures around the street corners but regretfully missed many others for lack of time.

Florence offered another feast to the senses. There I first learned about the Medici Family. (One American lady in the tour loved the Medici treasures in the Uffizi gallery so much that she asked if the articles in the art collection were for sale!) The Ponte Vecchio gave me a new perspective on covered bridges. Walking next to the Duomo, I was able to examine carefully the rich decorations of artfully fitted white, green and pink Tuscan marbles on the 276-foot tall Campanile wall. The bronze relief panels of Ghiberti's East doors in the Baptistry, commissioned in 1401 to mark the city's deliverance from the plague, were called the "Gate of Paradise" by Michelangelo and confirmed to me the genius of the Italian Renaissance. We rode horse-drawn carriages through ancient squares in Florence and enjoyed superb Tuscany cooking before going on to Venice.

Even though I grew up on the island of Hong Kong in a house at the water's edge, I could not imagine a city built entirely on water. That was Venice! All the houses stood in water, canals and bridges were the "city streets," filled with motorboats and the charming gondolas. The art collection in the city's museums dazzled me as did Venetian architecture. I cruised the canals, admiring the intricate decorations on old buildings as I listened to the gondolier singing his favorite operatic arias. I walked the narrow alleys and crossed numerous bridges, watched children chasing pigeons in remarkable St. Mark's Square and marveled at the art treasures in this famous aquatic city, saved from the sea for centuries through ceaseless human efforts.

My stop in Spain was also an eye-opener. In 1962, Franco was still in charge and the country appeared very poor, with many residents struggling to make a living. In Madrid, scars from the Civil War battles were visible on buildings and armed soldiers still patrolled the streets. I discovered the Prado's vast collection of Spanish painters and saw a Goya canvas for the first time. One must go to Madrid to see Goya's paintings, because the Spanish government has been reluctant to let them out of the country. The Alhambra was a delight and served as my introduction to Muslim architecture. Approaching the city of Toledo from a hilltop gave me an artist's view of the city, and a tour of its narrow streets, and charming houses with central courtyards reminded me of ancient Chinese houses.

Viewing the vast treasures of gold and gemstones displayed in the Spanish churches, I was overwhelmed with a sense of sadness. Through the centuries the church has collected tribute from its parishioners. Instead of improving the people's lives, however, the priests, bishops, cardinals and popes just kept this treasure for their own pleasure, building edifices and gathering jewels to "glorify God." The people kept suffering, still contributing to the riches of the church in the hope of a better life, clinging to the promise of an afterlife and perhaps of salvation. The church just kept accumulating. It was all so sad and senseless.

I finally arrived in Hong Kong in time for the joyous occasion of my father's birthday celebration. All nine of us siblings were there, the first time we had all been together since 1945. During the intervening decade and a half, we had all grown and changed greatly. Some were married and had children, most had been educated in the United States and received college degrees, some earned graduate degrees. We had attended America's famous universities: Princeton, Johns Hopkins, Columbia, Harvard, Swarthmore, University of Wisconsin, Temple University, Stanford and California Institute of Technology, and had become contributing members of both Hong Kong and American societies. Most of all, we had fulfilled the dreams of our parents, especially those of our mother. From an illiterate upbringing, she had educated her nine children successfully in the best universities in the world! This was a heady and happy moment for her. She smiled all day long, asked us questions, and offered advice and food as usual, still looking after our well-being.

The spacious house was never quiet, for we talked and argued from morning till night, indeed into the wee hours of the morning. We all cherished this rare occasion and wanted to make the most of it. Our parents just beamed and remarked how wonderful it was to have us all home.

On the morning of my father's birthday, we gathered in the large living room for the tea-offering ceremony to both parents. This traditional tea-offering was still practiced in our home, on Chinese New Year's Day as well as on our parents' birthdays. (A new bride coming into the family would perform this ceremony on her wedding day as a sign of acceptance by the family and as a symbol of submission to her elders.)

Two chairs were placed at one end in the living room for my parents. A red carpet lay in front of them. We all stood around the large room, waiting for our turn. One by one, according to the order of our birth, we each knelt, with our spouse if married, in front of our parents and kowtowed, touching our heads to the floor three times. Then, taking the tea cup from the maid's hand, we offered it to our father first, then to our mother, wishing them good health and longevity. The old tradition would require us to get up and kneel three times, but our parents were more modern and we knelt only once.

During this offering, advice and admonitions were customarily given by the elder recipient of the tea to the younger individual. Should the elder so choose, he or she could refuse the offering and publicly humiliate the younger person. But this seldom happened. The advice was usually along the lines of "work or study hard" and "stay healthy," not the "you were a bad person" type.

I remember the morning of my mother's sixtieth birthday, a couple of years later, as we proceeded to offer tea, the first ones to kneel were eldest brother Yingjim with his wife. After kowtowing and taking the tea cup from the maid's hand, he offered it to my father — always man first — then to my mother. But she refused to take it from him! Standing on the sideline, I was stunned to find myself listening to my mother scolding Yingjim for being selfish and not caring for his siblings, being greedy and egotistical. I knew the two of them did not always agree, but he was my mother's firstborn and favorite son and he was supposed to be a model for all the younger siblings to emulate. Even though Yingjim was no longer my mother's favorite child, for she had made her youngest, Yingbun, her favorite, how could she humiliate him like that in front of the whole family? Clearly, the admonition by my mother shocked Yingjim. He was heartbroken. I can still see him, a grown married man with his children watching, kneeling there with his wife, in front of our mother, sobbing loudly, asking what he had done wrong and begging for her forgiveness. I shall never forget that scene. We did have a severe and stern mother.

On this day however, my father's sixtieth birthday, everything went smoothly. After we offered tea, all received large good luck, red envelopes from my parents for the offerings, and everyone was happy. We had breakfast together and chatted more.

The rest of the day was dedicated to preparing for the banquet that night. The women had to have their hair done and get outfits ready. Jewels had to be fetched from bank vaults. The men tended to their daily business or made sure their tuxedos still fit them. Last minute preparations for the evening had to be made.

Invitations had been sent to family, friends and business associates. My parents by that time had prospered. They had donated to charities and served as board members on charitable organizations, therefore had a high standing in the community. Yingjim had served in the Hong Kong Legislative Council and was well known. Second brother, Yingchou, a cardiologist, though living in Detroit, had consulted and worked at the

Hong Kong University Medical School and remained friends with many professors there. Third brother Yingsheung, fourth brother Yingkwong and youngest brother Yingbun had all been involved with the property market working on housing development, and were well recognized in the community. People responded to the invitations well and gifts were arriving daily at my parents' house in Happy Valley.

The celebration banquet was held in a big Chinese restaurant. A thousand guests attended. A hundred round tables, each seating ten people, were set in the large banquet hall. We arrived early to greet guests that had come early to the restaurant to play Mahjong or other games, as was customary. We also visited with seldom-seen distant relatives.

Since these banquets never provide seating place cards for guests, most people came early and arranged to sit with their friends. Often, men sat with men at one table and women sat with women at another table. If sitting at a mixed table, a woman, being careful not to be too outspoken, would often go through the whole affair without speaking. She just sat there, smiled and looked pretty.

In the old days, Chinese musicians were hired to play loud and festive music, seemingly for the purpose of drowning out conversation. Tradition was that the louder the music, the happier the occasion. Nowadays, any hired musicians usually played quieter Western dancing music; seldom loud Chinese drums and gongs.

The guests were seated. Our family, in formal attire — the married women in their wedding dresses, resplendent with jewels; the men in their tuxedos — sat down together at two head tables, and the party started. Famous citizens and celebrities conveyed their congratulations, and laudatory speeches and toasts were given. The food and wine were then served.

A traditional nine-course banquet begins with one to four cold dishes and one to four hot ones for appetizers. When the waiter puts the dish on the center of the table, someone asks his neighbor or other prominent person at the same table to start. Everyone demurs. Finally, a person bold enough to begin starts serving his neighbors one by one, reaching over several persons sometimes, before he serves himself. All through the banquet, food is continuously passed from the center serving plate to the individual plates by people who urge everyone to eat more. It was the same at my father's banquet. I remember that I seldom had to help myself to any dishes in these banquets: someone was always there to serve me from the center plate.

After the appetizers, a whole roasted piglet was served with the crispy skin sliced into small squares. This dish is eaten with a small pancake, together with green onion and hoi-sin source; the rest of the piglet and the meat would be served later if ordered. This was a delicacy mostly served at formal occasions. A dish with abalone followed. This was made with reconstituted dried abalone, braised with chicken stock for a long time and served on top of green vegetables. These rarities could cost from a hundred dollars per abalone or more, depending on their sizes — the larger, the more costly.

Next came a sautéed dish with prawns. Then a Peking duck was served whole with the head on, but the meat on the bird was cut into small pieces and reassembled on the plate. Next, waiters served shark's fin soup in individual bowls at the table — shark's fin soup is served at formal occasions because it is costly. Then a whole fish appeared, prepared as always with the head on, followed by rice and noodles. The fish dish ensured that there would be plenty to eat (the word fish sounds like the word abundance), and noodles were a must for a birthday party for they signify longevity. For dessert, besides sweet soups, there was a small peach-shape bun, called "shao-tao," with a light pink coloring on top, and sweet stuffing inside. Shao-tao is always served at birthday celebrations, for the peach is also a symbol of longevity.

After the last course was served and a reasonable time had elapsed, someone stood up to signal the end of the celebration, and everyone left all at once. My whole family stood in line at the front door to say good-bye to our guests. I remember how tired my right hand was from shaking hands with them. It was a grand occasion.

During this visit I learned my father had followed the Chinese tradition of dividing his fortune to facilitate an orderly transition of his business interests and worldly possessions. Following a local accountant's advice, he had divided it among his five sons. I was surprised to hear that he had not bequeathed anything to his daughters, for I believed that my parents had treated all of us children, boys and girls, the same. Surely they had educated both the girls and the boys despite the old Chinese belief of educating only boys.

One day, while I was in the living room chatting with my father, I raised this question, asking him why he did not bestow some of his fortune to his daughters, too. He told me that it was a thousands-year old Chinese tradition that he could not do anything about. I was speechless. How could one argue with a father about the disposition of his fortune? After all, it was his money, his possessions, I had no right to it. But why did he treat his daughters differently from his sons? Somehow, this persistent Chinese favoritism for males gave me a warning that Hong Kong was not the place for me. I would not be willing to shoulder such prejudices.

I knew in my heart that this prejudice against women was historical and lies at the heart of Confucian doctrines, yet I could not accept it; not after I had studied and practiced my profession with men in the United States for so long and knew that I could do as well as any man could. It was extremely difficult indeed for me to tolerate this unequal treatment by my father, since he had always been so loving and gentle towards us, his daughters. I could not fault him for his beliefs, I could only blame it on the tradition he lived in. He obviously did not want to break this tradition which kept his fortune in the family. Fortunately, I was able to choose not to live under such social rules. I decided to return to the United States.

My mother, naturally, wished me to stay and marry in Hong Kong so she would have a daughter nearby. She asked me what I wanted in a husband. I told her I did not know exactly what I wanted but I knew that I could not marry any of these nice young men she had introduced and matched me with. She was disappointed and told me that I was too willful. However, she did not force me to marry as so many old fashioned Chinese parents did.

One day, on a Chinese religious holiday, she and I went to a temple to pay tribute to the gods, as she often did on such holidays. On the grounds of the temple, fortune tellers stood ready to predict anyone's fortune for a small fee. After we made our offerings to the gods, my mother suggested that we go to one of the well-known fortune tellers and ask to have my fortune told.

The fortune teller told me to choose a stick from the bamboo container in front of us. According to the number on the stick I picked, he produced a slip of yellow paper (yellow is considered sacred) with a poem on it. Since my quest was about whether I should live locally or go away, he explained that the poem, therefore the gods, said I would go away for a blessed life and much happiness would come my way. It was a beautifully written poem and I appreciated its literary value,

but the interpretation did not seem obvious. My mother, however, was convinced that fate had ordained me to live in faraway
places. She resigned herself and agreed to my return to the
United States. That was how she decided.

Before I booked my flight to San Francisco, an old friend,
Elizabeth, living in Manila in the Philippines, asked me to
come visit. She told me she and her husband were planning a
business trip to Sydney, Australia. Would I like to join them for
a short trip? The timing was perfect as I had not been to Australia. So before my return to San Francisco, I flew to Manila
and stayed at Elizabeth's spacious family compound with
swimming pool, lush gardens and all manner of help. Maids,
butlers, gardeners, chauffeurs and guards were discreetly stationed throughout the house and grounds. She gave me a complete tour of the city, so I also saw how the poor people of the
city lived. The difference between the rich and poor was stark,
like that in the Asian society I grew up in. Only now I was much
more sensitive and noticed it.

After a few days, we flew to Australia.

We were met at Sydney airport by my friend's business associates and were treated royally. They took us to the races and
the zoo, entertained us in their homes and the best restaurants.
I was surprised that we felt no trace of the then much-publi-
cized racial discrimination from Australians.

Sydney with its beautiful bay compared favorably with San
Francisco. Unlike San Francisco's townhouses and apartments,
however, Sydney's one-story, single-family homes surrounded
by beautiful gardens had a more suburban and English feel.
The weather is mild like San Francisco's but much less foggy. I
felt that if I could not live in San Francisco, Sydney would be
my next choice, though I don't like its isolation. One has to fly
a long way to get anywhere from Australia.

We also visited Melbourne. With its English-style architecture and store-fronts hanging with decorative, old fashioned specialty signs, Melbourne reminded me of Boston. It is also quieter than Sydney but did not have the incomparably beautiful bay around it.

I finally arrived in San Francisco, completing my round-the-world trip, and decided to make my life in California. I hired a commercial concern to bring my car and its contents from New York.

San Francisco was an ideal place for me to live. Californians seemed to be much more open and friendly than Bostonians or New Yorkers. Culturally, the Bay Area was much more diversified, and this diversity enabled me to enjoy my beloved Chinese cuisine. Besides being beautiful, San Francisco, at the time, had no traffic jams, few high-rise buildings; and best of all, it had better pay for pharmacists and a lower cost of living than New York City. I decided to make it my home.

· 21 ·

San Francisco

*T*he chief pharmacist of St. Luke's Hospital of San Francisco, Miss Marie Cook, was delighted when I showed up to apply for the advertised vacancy for a staff pharmacist in the hospital, for she had heard of Mrs. Evelyn Scott of the St. Luke's Hospital of Cleveland. We talked about how Mrs. Scott ran her pharmacy with an iron hand, what excellent standards were maintained and how she demanded the highest performance from her staff, who always practiced pharmacy according to the book.

Miss Cook told me: "If you could work for Mrs. Scott for three and some years, you must be a good pharmacist." She hired me on the spot with a salary much higher than the one I had received in New York.

With the help of my sister Waifong, I found an apartment in the Terra Vista district, on a hill right in the middle of San Francisco. The apartment was part of a duplex with large picture windows. I could see all the way to Mt. Diablo from one window and all of downtown San Francisco from another. The one thousand square feet consisted of a large living room, a dining room connected to the kitchen, and a bedroom with a full bath, a comfortable place.

Since the rent of one hundred and thirty dollars a month was quite reasonable, I decided not to find a roommate. For the first time in my life, I lived by myself. After years of living at home with siblings, in dormitories with school mates or in city apartments with other girls, I finally lived alone. It felt strange to have so much freedom and privacy. At first, I thought I would be lonely. Coming home to an empty house after work seemed sad and forlorn. Then I realized that I had felt lonely and forlorn even when I had roommates living with me. Now, I found solitude gave me time for reflection and sorting out my thoughts and feelings to better understand them. The calm environment enabled me, in fact, to think uninterrupted for long periods of time if I wanted to. Living alone also gave me a feeling of being more independent. I could decide what to do with all my time and energy, doing things I wanted to do instead of being dictated to. That was specially true for making friends and choosing social activities. So I began my new, independent life as a working young professional in San Francisco.

The work at St. Luke's Hospital was routine and not demanding. I went to work in the morning and came home after five o'clock, working only an occasional weekend. It left me with much energy to enjoy other activities. Routinely, after work, when I arrived home, I would put chicken pieces under the broiler and turn on the rice cooker, everything electric. Then I would draw a tub of water for a hot bath. By the time I was done with the relaxing bath, the rice and chicken would be done. All I had to do was to steam some vegetables and eat dinner. Many nights, though, I went out with friends and did not come home until quite late.

San Francisco was quiet compared with New York City: no traffic jams, no crowded streets. A clean city, beautiful with its hills and valleys — its forty-seven square miles felt almost like a small town. Besides many good restaurants, the city had wonderful sights and interesting surrounding areas to visit. The large Chinese population and the established Chinatown made me feel more at home than any other city in the United States I had lived in. Frequent visits to nearby Chinatown enabled me to enjoy authentic Chinese cuisine. I joined the Chinese Christian Association and even went to church a couple of times. The fellow members in this Association took me to Lake Tahoe and Sun Valley, and taught me how to ski at my advanced age of thirty-four! I also went with them to Monmouth Lake, Squaw Valley and other ski areas. We used to get up at four or five o'clock on Saturday morning, drive the three or four hours to the ski area in time for the opening of the lifts, then ski all day. Sometimes we drove back the same night; other times we stayed overnight and skied for another day, starting back after the lifts closed on Sunday. A whole week of skiing at Sun Valley, Idaho, made me an intermediate skier, enabling me to enjoy the sport heartily. Even though I came back with a sun-tanned face, looking like a raccoon, it was most enjoyable. I often wondered why my mother had objected to my taking skiing at the University of Wisconsin, saying it was a dangerous sport when I asked for her permission to do so. She did not subscribe to the idea that, like everything else, one just had to learn how to do it and then it would not be dangerous. Would I have become a better skier if I had started sooner? I would never know.

I made friends with fellow pharmacists as well. Many young professionals lived here in San Francisco. We gathered for the theater or a symphony concert as well as for dinners and the famous California gathering called a barbecue, where we cooked outdoors on a grill while chatting with friends. In the suburbs, this could be done all year around in the mild Bay Area weather.

Yet, for some reason, life was not going well for me. I felt sad without knowing why. My depression came back. I again felt that I had no purpose in life, no goal, nothing to strive for.

I found no joy in life, my profession did not satisfy me. I did not love my work, my social life, my surroundings, my friends or my family. I did not even love myself. A life without love could not be a happy one.

One night, alone in my apartment, I again decided to end my life. I had always kept a number of sleeping pills in my possession. Looking at the barbiturate capsules in front of me, I thought I should say good-bye to somebody. I thought of fourth brother, Yingkwong, who was living in Philadelphia and working for the Honeywell Corporation. I called Yingkwong and started to cry my heart out on the phone. He was one of the kindest persons in the family, and we had a close relationship growing up. I don't know why I wanted to say goodbye just to him and no other family members. Perhaps it was because he was the most sympathetic to my off-and-on depressions. My sisters, who lived nearby, could not understand why I was depressed, telling me that I had everything I wanted in life, what was there to be depressed about? They viewed my depression or suicidal thoughts as a means of drawing attention to myself.

I told Yingkwong life was not worth it, I might as well put an end to the pain. After a short conversation, he told me to hang up. Within minutes, a minister from some church in Philadelphia was on the phone trying to console me. He kept me on the phone talking for a long time, calming me down and eventually convincing me to give up the idea of killing myself. By the time I got off the phone, I was exhausted and finally fell asleep.

The next day, I realized that I must seek professional help. For the third time in my life, I was under the care of a psychiatrist. The Harvard-trained physician saw me once a week for forty-five minutes. I sat in his office and just talked about my childhood and how I grew up. Most of the time, I cried uncontrollably. He did not seem to know how to help me and did not prescribe any medication for me, though there were a few drugs available for depression at the time. My condition did not improve, but the sessions gave me a chance to talk with someone, someone who I thought knew about mental problems. I often wonder if an understanding, listening, good friend could have substituted for a psychiatrist.

Again, I thought perhaps changing jobs would help. It was depressing to work in the basement pharmacy doing the most routine work. There was little contact with people or the outside world except for a few fellow workers. After some searching, I had two job offers. One was as chief pharmacist at a small hospital in the East Bay in San Leandro, the other was as staff pharmacist at the Co-Op pharmacy on Shattuck Avenue near the University of California campus in Berkeley. I had trouble deciding which job to take so I discussed it with my psychiatrist. He thought that if I took the job in Berkeley, I would meet more people than I would in the hospital job. The Co-Op, a grocery store as well as a retail pharmacy, was a common meeting place for students and faculty of the University. At that time, the Berkeley campus was a gathering spot for liberal movements. There was never a dull moment. Many people gathered daily at the Co-Op near the campus, discussing issues and demonstrating. I would definitely see more people there. My psychiatrist's advice proved prophetic.

I had also learned of the Retail Clerks Union. Friends told me that pharmacists working in certain retail pharmacies, such as chain stores, were required to join the Union and received much better benefits than hospital pharmacists. The generous health and dental insurance, retirement provisions and other benefits made the membership worth the monthly dues. My friends urged me to work at the Co-Op and join the pharmacist's union. They also said it would be a more interesting place to work. I was hesitating about being a chief pharmacist in a hospital, even though that was what I was trained for, afraid that I would end up like Mrs. Scott. (That seems silly now, but it was a real concern at the time.) So I decided to take the job at the Co-Op, my first retail pharmacy job, commuting daily across the Bay Bridge from San Francisco and sharing the political excitement of the 1960s at Berkeley.

People in the pharmacy were extremely nice. The staff consisted of the black male chief pharmacist, two white male pharmacists, and me, no other helpers. The job did change my routine. Unlike hospital pharmacy, where the pharmacist dispensed patient medication in the bowels of the hospital and sent them to nursing stations for the nurses to give to patients, in retail pharmacy the pharmacist gave the patients their medications and talked to them, discussed their medication with them and answered their questions. Some patients brought their personal problems to us and we became friends. There existed much more human interaction in retail pharmacy. The store began to feel like a big family.

The Co-Op grocery store was indeed an exciting place to be. Young college students, retired professors, Nobel laureates and liberal hangers-on all came to shop. Demonstrations for various causes occurred daily outside the store. The store itself was owned by members who invested money in the establishment. Some owned a large number of shares, others just a few, but all had the right to comment on the administrative policies. Everyone walked around as if they "owned the place," and rightly so. The administration provided childcare centers for shoppers, and maintained an education booth filled with pamphlets on almost any subject, including food, nutrition, child-rearing, health issues, and crafts. A credit union for members held regular monthly meetings. Many issues were discussed in other organized meetings by members. One could feel the vitality of the University and indeed the whole East Bay in that place.

The Vietnam War was on, and most students at the University of California were against it. Students demonstrated daily. Newspapers published articles by mothers who complained about their sons, who were "brought up by pediatricians," being sent to die in the "rice paddies" of Asia. Since the draft system was still in effect, most young men would have to serve in the military at one time or another. Students staged draft-card burning rallies and protests to show how unjust the war was, both to Americans and to Vietnamese. Slogans such as "No, No, We Won't Go" and "Make Love, Not War" were chanted and posted everywhere. Most of the demonstrations were peaceful until the government started to use police and tear gas to disperse the demonstrators.

Personally, my depression did get better. I was able to hang on and functioned effectively in my daily life. Even after a night of partying or traveling late out of town, I was still able to discharge my duties as a pharmacist. Mine was not a profession in which one could make mistakes, and I prided myself on being a professional. That pride boosted my self esteem. Compared with the aimless, wild, and careless individuals I watched passing by in endless numbers, I felt that I, at least, was still doing something for society, not a parasite.

In addition to the pharmacy, the Co-Op grocery store also operated a coffee shop with counters and tables and chairs. I often sat at the counter for coffee breaks or lunch during the day. The food was good and the spot was convenient, right next to the pharmacy. Moreover, the friendly atmosphere was conducive to interesting conversations while we ate. One never knew if one were talking to a professor of classics or this year's Nobel laureate unless he or she mentioned it. These possibilities always made lunch an enjoyable and relaxing pastime.

One day in the spring of 1966, I was sitting at the lunch counter waiting to be served. As always, I had brought a book to read, and on this day, I was reading *The Sound and the Fury* by William Faulkner. I noticed a young man across the counter looking at me and I smiled back at him. Before I knew it, he was sitting on the stool next to me. We started a conversation about William Faulkner. I confessed that I did not know a thing about the author. This difficult novel and the unpronounceable names of its characters were impossible for me to comprehend. He told me that his undergraduate degree was in English Literature and he had indeed studied Faulkner. Since literature was also one of my favorite subjects, we immediately plunged into it with great interest. Besides telling me a good deal about Faulkner, he also mentioned books he had read recently. Among them was the *Pawn Broker*, which I had also read. The discussion became very lively, and we moved to one of the tables.

Soon my lunch hour was up and I told him I had to go back to work.

"Where do you work?" He asked.

I pointed to the pharmacy and said: "There. I am a pharmacist."

I went back to work happy that I had had an enlightening conversation. He did not ask my name nor did I ask his. That did not seem important.

Two days later, I was in the back filling prescriptions when a fellow pharmacist called and said: "Cynthia, here's someone to see you." I went to the customer window and recognized the young man with whom I had had the conversation about William Faulkner.

"Could we have lunch?" he asked.

I answered truthfully, "It's not my time for lunch."

"Maybe next time."

"OK," I said, and went back to work.

Nearly every day for the next few weeks, this young man would line up at the pharmacy window at noontime and ask to see the "lady pharmacist." Our exchange was always the same. He would ask if we could go to lunch, I would answer that it was not my lunchtime, and he would say "Maybe next time."

The other pharmacists began to notice this ritual and wanted to know what was going on. I finally confessed that my mother had forbidden me to go out with Caucasians and I did not think I should encourage this young man.

The chief pharmacist, Bill Harris, said, "Cynthia, don't give me this racial stuff. I went to the Second World War in our segregated Army; I know all about this nonsense of racial prejudices. He seems like a nice young man. You should at least go out with him once."

I quietly demurred.

The next time when the young man came to the window and asked me to go to lunch with him again and I gave my regular answer, Bill Harris shouted: "Cynthia, go to lunch now, I'll cover for you." Since he was the chief pharmacist, I was free to go. No more excuses.

We went to a nearby restaurant on Shattuck Avenue for lunch and talked some more. Finally, we introduced ourselves and I found out his name was Jonathan Wilcox and that he was a first year law student at the University of California's Boalt Hall School of Law. He was from North Branch, New Jersey, and I was only the second Chinese girl he had ever met. We enjoyed lunch and agreed to have dinner together the next night. I went back to work.

The next day, we had dinner at a small restaurant named Crouchon's in Berkeley. We talked and talked — actually, I did most of the talking, because he wanted to know all about me. In the midst of discussing literature and world politics, we were so totally engrossed in our conversation that when we finally stopped and looked around, we noticed the waiters were putting chairs upside-down on the tables, ready to clean the place. We were the only ones left in the restaurant. Reluctantly, we left. He saw me home and kissed me good night. Right then, I knew I had to marry this man. But how, how could I marry a Caucasian who was fourteen years my junior? I had to face reality.

· 22 ·
The Rules

*T*he announcements read: "Obeying the order of our parents, we have decided the marriage of our children." In China, in the Confucian tradition, marriages concerned families, not the two individuals involved. The decision was supposed to be made by the most senior living member of the family, be it parent or grandparent. A person, male or female, was to be married "following the order of his parents and the words of the marriage brokers." Besides bringing the child to adulthood, parents also had a duty to find a mate for him, not a mate the child likes or loves but one that makes sense to the parents, so that the child will "make a home and establish a family." The young people involved had very little to say about it. Confucians held that the greatest disobedience was "not to have an offspring" to carry on the family name. Having children married and having offspring was a man's duty. This contributed, obviously, to the importance of having sons.

In choosing a mate for their children, parents usually required that families be matching in social as well as financial status before they would talk marriage for their children. It had to be "bamboo doors to bamboo doors, and wooden doors to wooden doors." From the parents' experience and with society's approval, these marriages usually worked out. People of similar upbringing usually got along better in life. Marriage guidelines were not involved or concerned with matters of the heart but rather emphasized more practical principles such as wealth, health and prestige.

I was brought up in the Confucian ethics from a very early age. I had memorized the Four Books, the codes of conduct for Confucian scholars, in grade school. Without my realizing it, these rules and customs had become the basis of my conduct and thinking. My later education in the Western World, of course, introduced me to a different concept of marriage. So I also held the romantic notion that friendship, intimacy, and above all love, are important elements in a marriage.

I had always thought that these notions need not be in conflict with my basic thinking about obeying my parents in marriage. My parents did not order me to marry anyone they had chosen but had stipulated only that I should marry a Chinese. I was confident that I could find some Chinese to love who would be approved by my parents. Hadn't I been careful about whom I dated, mainly Chinese men of similar upbringing, so that in case the question of marriage should come up, I would get my parents' approval?

But in all these years I had not been able to find the right Chinese man. For all the times I had been dating Chinese men, I found most of them had ideas about marriage very different from mine. They seemed to have a formula: a Chinese girl, pretty, healthy, from a respectable family or similar background. Love and friendship, emotional intimacy or even knowing each other well, did not seem important to them. I had marriage proposals from Chinese students in college after only a few dates and we hardly knew each other.

I had accepted the Western ideals of marriage and insisted on marrying for love. Yet, at the same time, I lived within my parents' rules. Somehow, I did not see the conflict.

Now, my idea of marriage had come unglued! I had fallen

in love with someone. He did not match the Confucian idea of a mate: he was Caucasian, "not my kind," and younger than I was. I had to give up my long-held Confucian belief, my basic thinking and my obedience to my parents, or, alternatively, give up my idea of a marriage based on love and friendship. I was not willing to give up either. How was I to resolve the conflict?

Jonathan and I became very good friends and saw each other whenever we could. I was extremely happy finally to have found someone to talk with, to discuss life's puzzling problems with, to find out what life was really all about. Even though he did not have all the answers, at least we could talk, analyze pros and cons, compare historical and cultural perspectives. The fact that we came from entirely different cultures and family backgrounds made our conversations even more interesting and relevant.

I had come to live in the culture that he grew up in, and this adopted culture presented uncounted challenges to me. Ideas such as making laws to govern human conduct, all human conduct, seemed utterly impossible in my traditional mind. Society could be regulated only if everyone knows his or her traditional place in it and behaves accordingly. How can the government pass enough laws to put everyone in the proper place, to prescribe every behavior?

He, in turn, was interested in knowing the traditional Chinese culture, about which he had unending curiosity. These differences always brought up energetic, informative, stimulating and friendly discussions between us. Strangely, it seemed that we got along better because of our different backgrounds. We were never judgmental, just terribly curious about each other. We did not argue and there were no problems or issues we could not discuss amicably or intelligently. His gentle manners and lucid explanations made our discussions a great pleasure, brought joy to both of us.

My problems with depression often came up, and we thought perhaps it was because I felt that I had not fulfilled my mother's dream of my marrying a respectable family in Hong Kong. I felt guilty because I had always obeyed my mother. My worth was always measured by her approval.

Jonathan thought that I should be my own person, do whatever I wished, not what my mother wanted. Yes, I should get married, but for my own happiness, not to obey my mother. I should have my own family and companion for life. I told him I was confused as to what person to marry and would like some advice. He agreed to help. Thereupon, I introduced him to the four Chinese "beaus" I had at the time and asked him to select one for me.

Following my mother's requirements, Jonathan chose a newly-minted Ph.D. from the University of California, Berkeley, a plant physiologist about to take a position at a university in upstate New York. The young man's family wanted to see him married to a Chinese here before he went off to an area with few prospects. He seemed honest and had a healthy love for the outdoors. I could not see myself living in snowy upstate New York with an outdoors man, but I told myself I should not decide on the basis of residence. We had been dating for over six months but we rarely talked about ourselves and there was not a feeling of intimacy. He probably wanted to marry me because I fitted into the formula and I had the same reason to justify marrying him. Moreover, there did not seem to be anything "wrong" or undesirable about him. That was probably why I figured that I could adjust to life with him. My parents adjusted in their long marriage even though they had not met before their wedding day. I had no right to demand more.

After a few weeks, I received an engagement ring from the plant physiologist and showed it to Jonathan. He congratulated me and then, he told me later, went home to cry uncontrollably. He could not understand what was happening, he just fell sad with a great sense of loss.

But soon, knowing full well that I did not love this plant physiologist, I decided that I could not honestly marry him. I finally decided that even if I never married, that would be better than marrying someone I did not love, especially if we had children and then divorced. I gave the ring back and broke the engagement to the plant physiologist. I told Jonathan simply that I couldn't go through with the marriage, but I still confirmed the terms of my mother's requirements that I had to marry a Chinese. Jonathan tried to understand the situation, and he went to visit the plant physiologist, to encourage the fellow to try again. That visit, Jonathan told me later, made him realize suddenly that if this man could marry me, so could he, Jonathan. But, at the time, he had no plans to get married and did not know how to work all that out.

And I was still hoping: if I could only find a Chinese man to love and marry, my problems would be solved!

That summer, 1966, I was going to take my vacation visiting my parents in Hong Kong. The date was set and I had found another pharmacist to substitute for me during the extended time. Unexpectedly, Northwest Airline went on strike and all their flights over the North Pole to Asia were canceled. I told myself I was stranded and had to stay in San Francisco to wait for the strike to end. I was actually using the excuse to stay around, to be with Jonathan. We saw each other almost every day.

We visited various scenic spots around the area: Monterey, Big Sur, Napa Valley. One day, as we were about to go out my apartment door with cameras in hand, he suddenly took me in his arms and asked: "Would you marry me?" I could not believe what I heard and was totally flustered, dropping all my cameras.

Now, after all this time, he finally asked me! I could not believe it! He told me he knew that if he did not marry me, I would be gone forever. He wanted to be married now, regardless of his long-range plans.

After I collected myself, I found myself telling him:

"I can not marry you now."

I knew that my mother would disown me if I married a Caucasian. I had no illusions about that. Once I married Jonathan, I would not be welcome in Hong Kong nor in my parents' house.

"I have to go back to Hong Kong first. " I told him, "to see if I could live the rest of my life without the approval of my parents."

I can not describe the immense joy I felt. I had found someone to love, and he loved me in return. We could spend our lives together. I could marry the man I loved, Confucian ethics notwithstanding.

I was fully aware of other conventional issues: age difference, race, family background. But neither of us seemed to be bothered by how others viewed us. I had been told many times in the past about difficulties for people marrying Caucasians: social ostracism, discrimination against children. But Jonathan and I never saw each other as belonging to different races; we just saw each other as two human beings in love who wished to be married and have children.

True, I had been mindful and worried about my parents' approval, but I felt I was ready to deal with that: I was going back to Hong Kong to face it. If I felt that I had no problem living the rest of my life without my mother's approval, then I would come back to marry Jonathan. That would verify the fact that I was able to give up all the Confucian rules taught me long time ago.

· 23 ·

Marriage

As soon as the Northwestern Airline strike was over, I left for Hong Kong, with brief visits to friends in Seattle and Hawaii on the way. Hong Kong, I found, was getting ever more prosperous. My family was doing wonderfully well. Everyone was living a luxurious life, with maids and chauffeurs. I lived as they did and spent money the same way they did: "as if there were no tomorrow," as the saying goes. I bought expensive handbags, name-brand shoes and clothing, had dozens of outfits made by special tailors, and collected exquisite, rare designer jewelry. When I shopped in the United States, if a pair of shoes cost more than a hundred dollars, I would think twice before buying. Now in Hong Kong, with the large amount of money my parents put into my hands, I did not hesitate at all, as long as it was fashionable and beautiful. My whole concept of the value of money suddenly changed.

I stayed for two months, As usual, I shopped, visited with old friends and spent time with family, occasionally working as substitute pharmacist. It was a very leisurely existence amid the hustle and bustle of the crowded commercial city.

There was a certain standard of life style that I had to maintain, they told me. For instance, I could not go to the dirty market and shop for vegetables and meats for meals — only maids do that. I could not dress "shabbily" and be looked down upon by family and friends. People in Hong Kong judged a woman by how expensively she dressed — "respect the garment before respecting the person," they said. People made a point of knowing how much name-brands cost, and it was not out of place socially for a person to comment admiringly that one was wearing an extraordinarily expensive item.

However, life in Hong Kong seemed unreal and distant. People's concerns in life, mainly making money, were not mine. It was a totally different world from what I had imagined for my future life, not a world I wanted my children to grow up in. It was too competitive and shallow. I found few friends and acquaintances with similar interests. To me, the luxurious life style and the striving for fame and fortune seemed empty. I preferred the challenge of intellectual pursuits.

My parents' approval and love, which seemed indispensable to my happiness such a short while ago, was no longer necessary nor important to me. Now I had experienced another kind of love, the kind of love I felt secure in and could share, the kind I could appreciate, the kind that gave me support; not the materialistic, demanding, unfeeling sort that my parents meted out. I did not care about the jewels, fashionable clothing and worldly material things my parents gave me.

I came to realize that my parents had a different meaning of love. They loved me without even knowing who I was, what my aspirations were, what happiness meant to me. Their kind of love centered on forming and molding me to their ideal. They demanded that I obey them to meet their needs, not mine. They would like me to be well married so they could boast a wealthy or well educated son-in-law to give them "face." I was almost like a commodity to be traded. It was the traditional way for parents to view their children. Children had to be of "some use," children were brought up to "insure old age."

Surely, children should repay the parents' debt for bringing them up by following their wishes, obeying them.

I did not tell anyone, least of all my parents, about my pending marriage. I knew they would disapprove and perhaps even prevent my return to the United States, as they had, a few years back, when they learned of the intention of fourth brother Yingkwong's marriage to a Caucasian fellow student at Swarthmore College. They took away his passport and told the American Consulate that they would no longer sponsor his study or residence in the United States. They did not meet the girl he was to marry, nor ask him his reasons for choosing such a person. The fact that she was an American of the Caucasian race was enough for their disapproval. Eventually, with the support of friends, he did return, married and lived in the United States.

The day before I left Hong Kong, I told third brother Yingsheung that I was going back to the States to be married. He wanted to know who the person was. I admitted that he was a Caucasian, a first-year law student at the University of California, Berkeley.

"He is very young." Yingsheung said.

"I agree."

"Then you know what you are doing."

I assured him that, indeed, we knew what we were doing. He wished me luck, did not mention any concern about our racial differences, and took me shopping for my "dowry." I later learned that he was against interracial marriages, but he never mentioned it to me, perhaps not to offend me. I wish I had had a chance to discuss it further with him. He was the only one who knew my secret. I did not trust anyone else in the family with the news, for I fully realized how everyone felt about it.

However, I no longer felt guilty about marrying "not my kind." Confucius had preached that "if he is not my kind, his heart must be different from mine." I had found it untrue. I had been studying, working and living among these Caucasians, and I found that racial differences were superficial. To make the assumption that because people look different, they must necessarily think and behave differently was a gross, ignorant mistake.

Time for me to go back to the United States. It was very obvious to me that that was where my life belonged.

On my way back from Hong Kong, I stopped over in Seoul, South Korea, to visit a friend in the Chinese Consulate there. In the Fall of 1966, Seoul was very much a backwaters capital and had not recovered from the ravages of the Second World War. The road from the airport into the city was unpaved. The air conditioning in the best hotel in town was not working. When I ordered a beer at the large open-air terrace, the waiter brought out a liter bottle, not a can. I relaxed alone on the terrace and finished the whole liter by myself. The Korean people were very friendly to the few American and other tourists. Their temples and displays in museums reminded me of the close cultural relationship between the Chinese and Koreans. One museum in particular impressed me with its set of bronze musical instruments that dated back three thousand years. Watching a demonstration of these instruments, I began to understand how the ancient Chinese poets used the sounds from these bronze bells for rhymes. Also, I was most surprised to meet Koreans who still spoke and wrote Chinese after the repressive years of Japanese occupation of the prewar era. China's was a strong cultural tradition. Its hold on Asia would not diminish easily.

Anxious for my return, Jonathan could not wait for me to

arrive in San Francisco but instead, met me in Vancouver, Canada, my first stop in North America.

During the two months of my absence, he had grown a full beard — a large, red, Viking beard, his Norwegian heritage! When I first caught a glimpse of him at the exit gate waiting for me, my heart stopped. Had I come back to marry a "blue eyed, red-bearded devil?" What was going to happen to me? Did I make the right decision? Was this "foreign devil" going to abandon me like "Madame Butterfly" after we married? Was the age-old wisdom accumulated in Confucian teachings correct? Suddenly I was full of doubts, shaking in fear and anxiety, and the walk of a few yards toward the gate seemed like miles. But before I knew it, I was falling into his open arms.

As soon as we embraced, all that caution melted away. We were immersed in our own little paradise. My whole body was still shaking, but with excitement now. I could not say a word, all I could do was just hold on to him tightly. I would not let him go. In his arms, I felt happy and secure.

In early November 1966, Jonathan bought me an engagement ring at Tiffany's in San Francisco. I wrote home to tell my parents that I had become engaged to be married to a Caucasian man from New Jersey. Except for the fact that he was beginning the second year of law school and that we got along very well, I knew very little about his background. I had not met his family, did not know if they were rich or poor, honest or devious. Most important, he was good to me and we loved each other.

All hell broke loose in Hong Kong. My mother wrote back in her own almost illiterate handwriting, not through her secretary, asking: "How could you do this to me?" She continued: "You knew I disliked it, and you still did it! That's disobedience! Have you no filial love?" And she concluded:

"What will people think? You have brought shame to the family."

I wrote back that what people in Hong Kong thought had nothing to do with my life in America. I did not know them and they didn't know nor care about me. "It is my life," I told her, "I want to live it the way I see fit. I meant no harm to anyone. The people in Hong Kong should not be concerned about how I live my life. It was not my intention to disobey you." My letter had no effect. There was no use trying to explain to my mother that we loved each other, for she knew nothing about this kind of love. She would not be able to understand.

My younger sister said: "Don't do it. People will come and look at you as if you were an animal in the zoo!" I shouted back: "That's their problem. I would not be in the company of such people anyway."

When Jonathan's mother heard that her first-born son had decided to marry a Chinese girl, she lamented to her two younger sons: "I guess someday one of you will marry a black girl!"

I was told later by one of my brothers-in-law that he felt sorry for me. When I asked him why, he said: "How would you like to be Chinese all the time?" I told him that I liked it just fine. As a matter of fact, I was rather proud of it. He needn't feel sorry for me.

Occasionally, I did encounter discrimination in the United States, but I was seldom troubled by it. I found that the best way to handle discrimination was by ignoring it. If I did not agree that I was inferior, I was not inferior. Those who discriminated against me were wrong.

Jonathan started to look for an apartment for us in Berkeley. He found one that he liked and told the landlord that he would bring his fiancee to look at it later. When I showed up after work with him that evening, the man said that the apartment was already rented. What irony! My parents did not want me to marry Jonathan because he was not Chinese and the landlord did not want to rent to us because I was Chinese!

Through a real estate agent, we finally rented a place on La Loma Street in the hills above Berkeley, a small apartment behind the garage. Every morning we had the benefit of being awakened by the starting noise of the upstairs neighbor's car as he left early for work. But the apartment was close to the University campus and the Co-Op Pharmacy where I worked. With over a thousand square feet in total area and large windows on two sides, it felt roomy and comfortable.

A Chinese wedding was definitely out of the question. A traditional American wedding given by the bride's parents was likewise impossible. We could not go through all the decision-making of preparing for a big wedding anyway. Jonathan wanted to be married as soon as possible so neither of us would have a chance to change our minds, he said, laughing.

"Then let's get married before Thanksgiving," I replied, "so we will have special something to be thankful for."

On the morning of November 23, 1966, the day before Thanksgiving, (also the day Jonathan had to turn in an important paper for one of his courses), we gathered in the courtroom of a judge in the Alameda County Court House in Oakland. Jonathan's roommate Eric Bauersfeld and my fellow pharmacist Bill Harris both took time off work to be our witnesses. I wanted Bill to be my witness because he had something to do with my dating Jonathan.

When the four of us — a black man, a Chinese woman and two Caucasian men — stood in front of the judge, he surveyed the unusual sight and said:

"Well, I guess you know what you are doing!"

Of course, we knew what we were doing! I suspected that Jonathan and I were probably the only two people at the time who could answer him affirmatively. Most people thought we were crazy to get married.

Seeing that nobody walked out, the judge went ahead and conducted the short ceremony. Jonathan and I promised to love and cherish each other for better or worse till death, and so became husband and wife legally. Everyone, including the judge, congratulated us. As fairy tales would have it, we have lived happily ever after.

Following the wedding, there was no honeymoon because of school and work. We had only a small lunch reception for a handful of close friends at the Claremont Hotel in Berkeley. We did not think of telling any one about our ceremony. Bill Harris could not even attend the lunch: he had to go back to work at the pharmacy.

Jonathan's mother wanted to give us a reception in New Jersey so members of the family could meet me. We decided that the only convenient time would be during the Law School's spring break. The reception would be held in the hilltop house of a close family friend in Green Brook, New Jersey. We sent his mother's invitations to family and friends and invited them to come celebrate with us. The invitation also served as notice that we were married.

We flew to Newark, New Jersey, in late January 1967, stopping in Detroit so my second brother Yingchou and his family could meet Jonathan. Attending the dinner Yingchou gave for us were some of my high school friends that lived nearby, including my old friend Yu Shumen and her husband Bob. The conversation was cordial and I never heard any comments about Jonathan or our interracial marriage.

From Newark airport, we took the bus, carrying our own

THE LOVE OF LOTUS

luggage, to his mother's house. That was an unusual experience for me, for I seldom took public transportation. Here was Jonathan with his new wife coming home to visit his family. Wasn't there anyone to meet us? Didn't they have a car or a chauffeur to drive us these long miles to North Branch? I kept these questions to myself.

The next day, Jonathan showed me around the small town of North Branch where he had grown up. We visited the old fashioned general store and the gasoline station where he worked when he was in college. When Jonathan introduced me to Pat, the owner of the gas station, I said hello and we exchanged a few pleasantries.

Pat exclaimed, "She even speaks English!"

I was immediately rendered speechless. I suppose he thought I was a "war bride," like so many brought back from the Orient or Europe, who hadn't learned to speak English yet.

My friends from New York and Boston, as well as my fourth brother Yingkwong and his Caucasian wife Sara, who were living nearby in Philadelphia, came to the evening reception. No one else in my family came. I was introduced to Jonathan's extended family, his grandfather and his Norwegian grandmother, his great-aunt Cora, his Uncle Bob and Aunt Alice and various other family members and friends. The informal reception lasted into the wee hours of the morning. If any disapproval or misgivings about our marriage existed in the minds of the guests, I did not notice it.

While we were visiting New Jersey, Aunt Cora went on a drive with us one day. She had never been married and at this time was in her seventies. Jonathan told me that he used to go to the graveyards to help her research the family genealogy when he was in high school, and that she believed she had found some very prominent ancestors in the Wilcox family, including William Shakespeare, before the ancestors left England on the Mayflower. The whole family regarded Aunt Cora as their matriarch and indulged her in her idiosyncrasies.

As we drove around the New Jersey countryside, she pointed to various landmarks and told me:

"Those great houses used to belong to our ancestors." She named several of them and described how they lived on their big estates.

"They had many black servants and numerous slaves working the fields," she proclaimed enthusiastically. "Some day, we will get all this back!"

Imprudently, I asked: "Aunt Cora, where will we get the black people and slaves to serve us and work the fields?" I had never learned the art of indulging old people and their fantasies. She stopped telling me stories about the family.

For some reason, after we got married, I decided that I needed a house, even though the year before when my mother came to visit, I had refused her offer to buy me a house on Marina Boulevard in San Francisco. "I don't want to be burdened with a house," I had told her. Now, all of a sudden, I needed one! Perhaps it was what was known as the "nesting instinct." Perhaps it was because now I knew I would "settle down." Perhaps , also, it was because now that I had a husband, I would have someone to care for and to share the house. It was a strange state of mind that to this day I do not understand.

After looking at only two houses, I began to despair that I would ever find the right one. Such was the urgency I felt. But luck was with us, and we bought the third house we looked at.

The large house was located in the Berkeley Hills, on Parnassus Avenue, facing west toward the San Francisco Bay. We fell in love with its magnificent view of the Golden Gate Bridge as soon as we walked in, even before we looked at the five bedrooms and the rest of the house. It cost forty thousand dollars. We put ten thousand dollars down and borrowed thirty thousand dollars for thirty years with a monthly payment of two hundred and two dollars. With my pharmacist's salary and Jonathan working part time at KPFA radio station, we could live reasonably well.

I felt that I was truly loved for the first time. It was like being a child again, secure in the world. It did not matter even if the whole family did not love me any longer, I had Jonathan, my partner for life. I believed that there was nothing we could not face together. I found that a most pleasant state of mind.

I had never felt so secure nor been so happy. We worked and studied, finding out about each other and celebrating our harmonious living relationship together. We hardly saw friends or family — the world was just the two of us, in our own little paradise. Jonathan seemed to have fulfilled all my needs so well that I did not need other human beings. I had never experienced such a close, intimate, comfortable, undemanding and pleasant relationship. For the first time since my life was disrupted by the invasion of Hong Kong by the Japanese on December 8, 1941, I felt the same peace, security and happiness of my childhood. I still had occasional depressions and anxiety spells, but they became much rarer and more controllable. When family members called or wrote to castigate me or my marriage, I suffered severely. But Jonathan was always there to hug and reassure me.

· 24 ·
Berkeley

O ne day early in 1967, Jonathan told me he did not want me to be just working to support us as so many American wives were doing so their husbands could go to college or graduate school. He wanted me to go back to school with him and share the experience at UC Berkeley. After what had happened at Harvard, I was not about to pursue any more graduate studies in pharmacology, biology, or pharmacy. Or any subject, for that matter. I had had enough of academic pursuits.

"You could study something you like," he suggested.

Something I liked — what a novel idea! I had never studied something I liked: I only studied things useful and pragmatic.

Almost impulsively I said, "Literature, that is what I would like to study."

I had always been envious of Jonathan's undergraduate study of literature and wished I had done that. How wonderful it would be if I could study English literature and share all that with him!

He then recommended: "Go to the University and see what they have."

Aware of my limitations in the English language, I decided perhaps I should study Chinese literature. So I made an appointment with the Chinese Department at University of California and asked about enrolling in the graduate school. At the meeting, the head of the department told me that my Chinese was not good enough. (He didn't say my English was not good enough.) He suggested that I should go to the Asian Studies Department and see if they would take me. I supposed there must be many students in the Chinese department who could recite Tang poems and the *Analects* or the *Four Books* from memory in Chinese better than I could!

Concealing my injured pride, I went to inquire about the program on Asian studies as directed. After a short discussion with the representative there, I learned that the Asian Studies Institute integrated and researched fields of anthropology, history, economics, law, art, literature and political science in Asia. To be able to connect and integrate all these fields together in the region seemed a most interesting undertaking.

She advised me to apply just to study and work on the subjects but not for a graduate degree, because they were short on funding for degree candidates. That suited me fine. I was not sure whether I really wanted a degree anyway.

So I applied to the Asian Studies Institute of the University of California at Berkeley as a graduate student, not a degree candidate.

Surprisingly, I was accepted, to start in the fall quarter of 1967. We could spend the last year of Jonathan's law school on campus and share the experience as he had desired. In the meantime, I would continue working at the pharmacy full time, mostly on weekends and evenings so I could take my courses during the week. The pharmacy staff were happy that someone was willing to work those hours and made schedules to accommodate me.

I chose to take courses on East Asia: China, Japan and Korea. Each course was taught in a separate department under famous professors. I had political science courses in the

Political Science Department, history and sociology in the History Department, law in the Law School (Jonathan took the Chinese Law course with me), anthropology in the Anthropology Department. The subjects were all very familiar to me. I found it exciting to study topics that I had learned earlier in Chinese. It was fascinating to learn the academic as well as the Western point of view.

My understanding and knowledge stood out in seminars and examinations without any effort on my part. I had never found courses so easy, and I enjoyed them tremendously! I also discovered the study of anthropology. The required reading and examination were easy compared to science courses. To learn about a society's customs and traditions, to me, was an interesting way to understand that specific culture. I also learned the way social scientists approached their subjects.

But studying and working was not enough for us. We wanted more out of living! We now wanted a child.

Before we were married, I went to a gynecologist, Dr. Minkler, to have a physical examination and to check on my general health. He pronounced me fit to be married. I asked about having children and he advised that I should wait for a year so Jonathan and I could adjust to each other before taking on the task of caring for an infant.

I questioned: " Should I wait even at my age?" I was then thirty-seven years old.

He said: "Yes, you should still wait for a year."

Innocently, we followed the doctor's orders and waited. But as soon as the year was up in November 1967, we decided to have children.

Without much trouble, our wishes were granted. By January, 1968, I was happily pregnant. Our spirits were high even though we were very busy. I was working and taking courses, and Jonathan was also working and studying. We shared our interests and rejoiced in our good fortune. There was not much time for social life other than an occasional dinner with good friends. We were happy and content with the world and we had a child to look forward to.

I cooked dinner every evening, and after we ate we talked for a while, did homework or watched the news on television. By eight or nine o'clock, I would be asleep on the sofa while Jonathan continued studying at the dining table. The hormonal change in my body due to the pregnancy made me cheerful at all times. Even though I was physically tired and slept a great deal, I was radiant and joyful throughout all those months. There was no horrible morning sickness, no depression; I only felt happy and tired all the time.

It was unfortunate that we did not know before my pregnancy that the hormones, possibly estrogen or progesterone produced by the body during normal pregnancy, could have eased my depressions. I could simply have taken birth control pills, which contained these two hormones, to keep away that demon. If we had only known. Health professionals did not seem to realize then that depressions might be a result of hormonal imbalances. And I did not believe in taking pills as a method of birth control. I did not think I should "disturb" my normal hormonal system!

The year 1968 was, to put it mildly, an eventful year in Berkeley as well as in the political history of our country. The Vietnam War was still on, American soldiers were dying in Asian rice paddies, newspapers published the "body counts" daily. Antiwar protests were everywhere and occurred almost daily on the Berkeley campus. Induction centers were destroyed, downtown Berkeley shops were regularly vandalized and wrecked. Shops on Telegraph Avenue were barricaded.

Police arrested large numbers of people and even sprayed tear gas on the Berkeley campus by helicopter in an attempt to disperse demonstrators. At night, we would often hear loud explosions nearby and the next morning would read in the newspaper that a certain gate or electrical tower on campus had been bombed by antiwar radicals the night before.

The country was in chaos, fractured by an unjust war. President Lyndon Johnson called up the reservists early in the year, then announced later that he would not accept the nomination of his party for another term in office, and "would not run, if nominated," after Senator Eugene McCarthy ran against the war in the New Hampshire Democratic Party primary. The non-violent black leader, Martin Luther King, Jr., was assassinated. In June, Bobby Kennedy was killed the night he won the California Democratic Party Primary in Los Angeles. At the Democratic Party Convention in Chicago, Mayor Richard Daley sent police on horseback to club and disperse Democratic Party delegates from the Eugene McCarthy campaign gathered in front of the Convention. These delegates were barred from the Convention.

National Guardsmen were called in to restore order on several campuses in the country and to put down student demonstrations. Everywhere people were opposing authorities and the war in Vietnam with revolutionary fury. A few times we joined a protest, to demonstrate against government policies.

The military draft system was still in effect. Every American man over eighteen had to serve in the Armed Forces for a time. Jonathan had received deferment from the draft when he entered law school, but we knew that as soon as he graduated, in June 1968, he would be called to serve. At that time, many young people of draft age made the decision to move to Canada to avoid the draft. From my antiwar point of view, that was better than going to Vietnam to be killed for no justifiable reason. We discussed the possibilities. I told him that I had already given up two countries, Great Britain and China. Giving up a third one probably would not be any great hardship for me. I thought I could handle it. Besides, in Canada we would still be living in a Western democratic country.

Standing on our balcony, looking toward the magnificent Golden Gate Bridge, Jonathan told me: "This is my country. I will not let anyone run me out of it. We are staying here." He refused to go to Canada.

In late May, I found that I had passed all the required courses for a Master's Degree in Asian Studies in the three quarters I had enrolled. In order to receive my Master's Degree, the only other requirements were a thesis and a language examination.

When I went to my adviser in the Anthropology department to take the language examination, he asked me: "You know Chinese, do you?"

I said: "Yes, that's my first language."

He passed me for the requirement without either one of us speaking a word of Chinese.

Then I asked him about the thesis.

Looking at my protruding midriff, he said: "You could take a comprehensive examination on East Asia instead of writing a thesis if you so choose."

That sounded much simpler, especially since my future plans at the Institute were rather uncertain: I didn't know if I had time to do research and write a thesis.

A week later, I took the comprehensive examination and was told that I passed "with flying colors." I had now met all the requirements and was duly granted the Master of Arts degree in Asian Studies!

We went to graduation ceremonies at both the Law School and the School of Letters and Sciences. Jonathan received his Juris Doctor degree and I, together with my unborn baby, received the Master of Arts degree. No family members came to celebrate with us, and I had a feeling that the family had "written us off." However, we did go to the reception on the lawn in front of Boalt Hall School of Law and had a chance to thank some of the professors and the dean.

Jonathan looked splendid in his academic black gown with three purple stripes on both sleeves. I thought to myself: "He should be a judge. His temperament fits that role. This country needs someone who's fair and just." But that was just my wishful thinking. I had no idea what our future would be like.

There were many unanswered questions: What was I to do with the degree I had just earned? What was Jonathan going to do with his degree, and the draft board? Would our baby be born healthy? Would Jonathan be drafted? Would he be killed in Vietnam and I left behind to raise our infant baby alone? Would I be able to work? Even if he were not drafted, would he be able to find a job? So many questions and so few answers. It was an end of a special period in our lives and the beginning of a most uncertain time.

· 25 ·

A Son Is Born

*A*s expected, the letter for Jonathan to report for a
physical examination soon came from the Draft
Board. He passed the physical examination and was classified
as "1-A," for immediate induction into the armed services.

Jonathan thought he might like to enroll in a military language training course in Monterey, California, so he would be
close by for at least a while longer. He went to the Army recruiting office near campus and arranged to take a language
aptitude test. A short while afterwards, the recruiting sergeant
told him that he had gotten a superb score. For a few moments,
Jonathan was thrilled. Then the sergeant said that the class
openings would be filled early the next morning as recruiters
phoned in the candidates' names to the Pentagon, and that
Jonathan's chances weren't good because the class probably
would be filled by applicants in the Eastern time zone by the
time his name was called in. Jonathan left, crestfallen. Much
later, it dawned on him that perhaps if he had been worldly
wise enough to offer a small reward to the sergeant to get up
extra early in the morning to make that call, he might have had
a better chance. We will never know whether that could have
happened.

By the middle of summer, Jonathan fully expected to go
into the Army, and he did not want me, more than six months
pregnant, to live alone in the house in the Berkeley hills.

Knowing my eldest sister, Waijin, lived in San Francisco, he asked if she could keep an eye on me if he should be called up by the army. Could she possibly help to care for the newborn baby when I delivered? Waijin agreed. But she asked that we move to San Francisco to be closer.

In August, we found a small, one-bedroom apartment on Taylor Street, close to where Waijin lived with her husband and two children on Lombard Street. Taking some furniture and other essentials to the apartment, we stored the rest of our belongings in a basement room. Leaving our house to five students from the University who rented it for the next year, we moved to San Francisco. There I found a job with the Pacific Medical Center Hospital pharmacy on Clay street in Pacific Heights and started working right away. Jonathan felt much better that I would be in a hospital working instead of at home in case anything should happen to me or the baby.

The call for Jonathan to report for duty had not come, but he could not find employment because of his 1-A status. Anticipating the birth of our baby, I was grateful to have him home. In order to have some income, he took on various temporary jobs as secretary, sales clerk, and delivery man. In his spare time, he continued to study for the Bar Examination. We tried our best to endure in this uncertain time, not knowing when and if he would be called, when our baby would be born and if our baby would be healthy.

Yet, even with all these uncertainties, I did not experience any depression. I maintained my cheerful mental outlook throughout. There were seldom moments of despair. Deeply in love with Jonathan as he was with me, I felt life was good to us and everything would work out as long as we were together. Surprisingly, I managed not to worry about what I would do if he were sent to Vietnam and died there. I told myself that I could face that too should it happen. My healthy mental attitude surprised both of us. Meanwhile, as I happily waited and prepared for the arrival of our new baby, I had no, or very little, idea what was involved in being a mother.

I had never baby-sat anyone in my life, never changed a diaper nor fed a tiny baby. My younger brothers and sisters were all cared for by maids when I was growing up. Then I went away to boarding school. The summer in Shaoquan where I had helped to care for youngest brother Yingbun was short and I was not alone. My older sisters and my mother were always there to change diapers and feed him. My concept of motherhood was mostly unreal and romantic.

As recommended, we took courses in natural childbirth and how to care for a newborn. At the Red Cross offices on Van Ness Avenue in San Francisco, we had a class on how to change diapers. When the instructor put a life size doll in my hands and started to put a cloth diaper underneath it to show how it should be done, I suddenly started giggling aloud and couldn't stop. It seemed to me that this was all playtime, something very unreal, and it was silly for me to be playing with dolls. I had never had such an experience before. The instructor was taken aback and told me there was nothing funny about changing a diaper. Once again, I had taken on a serious task without fully realizing its scope. Fortunately, as always, Jonathan was there to bail me out: he patiently showed me how to diaper the doll.

My water broke on the morning of October 18, 1968. Jonathan drove us across the Bay Bridge to the Alta Bates hospital around eight o'clock in the morning. My doctor lived in Berkeley and practiced at Alta Bates. Driving across the Bay Bridge, I tried to calm Jonathan's nerves by reassuring him all that time that I was fine, and the baby was not coming yet.

A Son Is Born

At the hospital, the nurses put me in the labor room immediately. Jonathan stayed with me, soothing and comforting me, enduring the painful screams I made as each contraction arrived, helping to relax me as they had instructed us in class. This went on for hours, sweat pouring down my forehead as fast as Jonathan could wipe it off. We were hoping for a natural birth without using any medication.

After helping me labor all day without much success, the doctor finally said at around nine o'clock in the evening: "I don't think you can give birth by yourself. We will have to perform a Caesarean section." With tears in my eyes, I told him: "Be sure to find the best surgeon possible." I had no idea what was going to happen. My hope and faith rested totally with modern medicine and the doctors. We both felt completely helpless, unable to control events.

They wheeled me into the operating room and gave me caudal anesthetics to help numb the pain in the lower part of my body. But I was aware of all the goings-on in the room. Jonathan was not invited to the operating room and he had to wait outside. The Caesarean section did not seem to take long and I did not feel pain any more. I was given oxygen, "to help the baby," the nurse said.

Soon, the cry of an infant was heard. When the nurse told me: "You have a healthy son," and showed me his perfect hands and feet, it was in the wee hours of the next morning. Looking at the tiny creature's long fingers and perfect face, I said to him: "You are a rascal for giving me such a hard time!" Jon Anthony was born on the early morning of October 19, 1968!

"Congratulations, Daddy!" I said to Jonathan when he visited in the recovery room.

It had been almost twenty-four hours since we arrived at the hospital and we were both exhausted. I told Jonathan to go home to get some rest. Yet he would not go, but kept telling me to "wriggle my toes." For a little while, I was totally confused. Why was he worrying about my toes? He wanted to make sure that the anesthetics did not have any untoward effects on the lower part of my body. After he was assured and I fell asleep, he drove home to San Francisco alone.

We began a new phase of our lives together. Now there were three of us. The focus of our lives would center completely on the tiny human being we had created. Little did I realize how completely our lives would be changed by this momentous and happy event.

A few days after I came home from the hospital with the new baby, I got up one morning and declared: "I am going to work." I started to walk across the room, my legs gave way and I collapsed on the floor before I could reach the door. Jonathan picked me up carefully and explained that life was going to be different. Perhaps I would not be able to do all the things I used to do.

"Not be able to go to work?" I asked incredulously.

He explained that I needed rest, to heal my wounds from the Caesarean section. Perhaps, after I recovered, I could return to work. I lay there motionless on my bed, contemplating taking care of a tiny helpless creature with my weakened body, not being able to go to work.

Miraculously, my body recovered, at least somewhat. Two weeks before Christmas, I was able to drive to the post office to send some gifts. That evening, Jonathan came home from work and I told him what I did.

He asked: "What did you do with the baby?"

"I left him in the car and locked the doors."

Horrified, Jonathan told me that I should never, never, ever leave the baby alone in the car.

"A baby could suffocate!" He cried: "There would not be enough air in the car for him to breath, enough oxygen for him to survive." Nobody ever told me, I never knew that!

Indeed, our world had changed. A son had been born to us. The tiny little creature depended entirely on our care. I never had had such important and constant demand placed on me. We could not be negligent even for one moment. We would have to be vigilant and alert all our lives. Being a pharmacist, dispensing the right medication to patients, was as important and as vital to the patients' welfare, but I did not have to perform that duty constantly. Furthermore, I was well trained for that duty, with built-in checks for errors. Now, I was doing this without any training or experience, learning as I went along, not knowing how to be a good parent. This job of parenthood must be the biggest challenge anyone could face.

Magically, with the attention and care we gave, our son grew strong and healthy, bringing us the great joy of watching a human being grow.